Grateful,
Caffeinated,
and Held Together by Grace

~ A 52-WEEK DEVOTIONAL BIBLE STUDY ~
GRATITUDE DEVOTIONS FOR
REAL CHRISTIANS LIVING MESSY LIVES

GRACE ANDREWS

© Copyright 2025 by Grace Andrews

All Rights Reserved

Grateful, Caffeinated, and Held Together by Grace

A 52-Week Devotional Bible Study

Gratitude Devotions for Real Christians Living Messy Lives

The content contained within this book may not be reproduced, duplicated or transmitted without direct written permission from the author or the publisher.

Under no circumstances will any blame or legal responsibility be held against the publisher, or author, for any damages, reparation, or monetary loss due to the information contained within this book, either directly or indirectly.

Scripture quotations taken from The Holy Bible, New International Version® NIV®

Copyright © 1973, 1978, 1984, 2011 by Biblica, Inc.

Used with permission. All rights reserved worldwide.

Legal Notice:

This book is copyright protected. It is only for personal use. You cannot amend, distribute, sell, use, quote or paraphrase any part, or the content within this book, without the consent of the author or publisher.

Disclaimer Notice:

Please note the information contained within this document is for educational and entertainment purposes only. All effort has been executed to present accurate, up to date, reliable, complete information. No warranties of any kind are declared or implied. Readers acknowledge that the author is not engaged in the rendering of legal, financial, medical or professional advice. The content within this book has been derived from various sources. Please consult a licensed professional before attempting any techniques outlined in this book.

By reading this document, the reader agrees that under no circumstances is the author responsible for any losses, direct or indirect, that are incurred as a result of the use of the information contained within this document, including, but not limited to, errors, omissions, or inaccuracies.

ISBN 978-1-7638974-9-6 (Paperback)

ISBN 978-1-7643432-0-6 (Hardback)

Hey God, I'm here—coffee in one hand, to-do list in the other.

Help me slow down enough to notice You in the chaos.

Speak truth and gratitude into my messy brain.

I'm listening, kind of overwhelmed, but ready.

TABLE OF CONTENTS

Introduction	1
Week 1: Grateful for Fresh Starts	4
Week 2: Meeting Me in My Mess	7
Week 3: Caffeinated Morning Prayers	10
Week 4: When Gratitude Feels Fake	13
Week 5: Grateful for Permission to Not Be Okay	16
Week 6: Thank You for Ordinary Days	19
Week 7: Finding God in the Daily Grind	22
Week 8: Grateful AND Grieving	25
Week 9: Thank You for Crying With Me	28
Week 10: Coffee Cup Communion	31
Week 11: Grateful for Friends Who Get It	34
Week 12: When Life Doesn't Match Expectations	37
Week 13: Thank You for Small Mercies	40
Week 14: Grateful for Growth That Hurts	44
Week 15: Thank You for Unanswered Prayers	47
Week 16: Finding Joy in Being Known	50
Week 17: Grateful for Second Chances	53
Week 18: Thank You for the God Who Sees	56
Week 19: Celebrating Tiny Victories	59
Week 20: Grateful for Grace in Relationships	62
Week 21: Through, Not Around	65
Week 22: Finding God in Waiting Rooms	68
Week 23: Grateful for Imperfect Families	71
Week 24: Thank You for Midnight Mercies	74

TABLE OF CONTENTS

Week 25: Celebrating Who I Am, Not What I Do	77
Week 26: Gratitude for the Work in Progress	80
Week 27: Rest for Weary Souls	84
Week 28: Thank You for Messy Kitchens and Full Hearts	87
Week 29: Finding Grace in Chaos	90
Week 30: Grateful for Bodies That Carry Us	93
Week 31: Laughter is a Gift From God	96
Week 32: Celebrating Ordinary Moments	99
Week 33: Grateful for Hard Conversations	102
Week 34: Thank You for Forgiveness	105
Week 35: Finding Joy and Gratitude in Simple Pleasures	108
Week 36: Grateful for the God of Details	111
Week 37: A Morning of Love and Grace	114
Week 38: Celebrating Progress, Not Perfection	117
Week 39: Grateful for Grace in the Storm	120
Week 40: Thank You for Lessons in Disguise	124
Week 41: Grateful for Changing Perspectives	127
Week 42: Finding God in the Darkness	130
Week 43: Thank You for Imperfect Celebrations	133
Week 44: Grateful for What Didn't Happen	136
Week 45: Celebrating Hope That Endures Long Waits	139
Week 46: Thank You for Chaotic Love	142
Week 47: Grateful for New Beginnings	145
Week 48: Maintaining Hope When Life Feels Stuck Or Broken	148
Week 49: Thank You for Faithful Friends	151

TABLE OF CONTENTS

Week 50: Grateful for Dreams Deferred	154
Week 51: Celebrating the God Who Stays	157
Week 52: Thank You for Grace That Never Ends (and Caffeine, too)	160
Thank you for reading	163
What's Next?	164
Get your FREE email mini-course 'The Grace-Filled Life'	165
About the Author	167

Introduction

Real life doesn't look like a greeting card sentiment or feel like a highlight reel from Saturday morning. It's messier than that. It's filled with burned dinners, tough conversations, unexpected detours, and situations that test every assumption you thought you had about faith, family, and the future. Yet somewhere in the chaos of ordinary days, gratitude grows, not despite the mess, but because of how God shows up for us.

This devotional was written for people whose lives don't fit into neat categories or follow predictable patterns. You might be navigating job changes at fifty, parenting adult children who make choices that break your heart, caring for aging parents while managing your health concerns, or simply trying to find meaning in a life that feels more like survival than celebration.

Gratitude doesn't demand that we pretend everything is fine or force joy we don't feel. When we open our eyes to God's faithfulness, we recognize His presence in ordinary moments and extraordinary challenges alike.

These fifty-two weeks will be about the kind of gratitude that acknowledges pain without being defined by it, hope that endures long waits, and grace that proves sufficient for whatever each day brings.

Each week focuses on a different aspect of grateful living—from celebrating imperfect friendships to finding purpose in delayed dreams, from receiving comfort in suffering to offering forgiveness when it costs more than you want to pay. The devotions are honest about the struggles we face in life. They're practical without being simplistic and they encourage without minimizing real difficulty.

You'll find no picture-perfect advice here, no suggestions that work only for people whose lives are already manageable. Instead, these pages offer the kind of hope that sustains you through 3 AM worries and overwhelming Tuesdays, the grace that covers your failures and empowers your fresh starts, and the community that stays when others scatter.

This devotional is for Christians who are still figuring things out daily, who need reminders that God's love doesn't depend on having a perfectly put-together life. Whether you're starting your day with coffee and prayer, or ending it with exhaustion and gratitude for simply making it through, this devotional is here to remind you that grace covers it all.

Some weeks will resonate deeply; others might feel like messages intended for the future or past version of you. Take what serves your soul today and trust that God will use other insights when you're ready to receive them. The goal isn't perfect understanding, but gratitude and authentic connection with God.

So grab your coffee or tea, find a comfortable spot, and prepare to discover gratitude that's big enough for real life. The messy, beautiful, challenging, grace-filled reality of being human. You're held together by more than simply determination or good intentions. You're held together by grace, and that changes everything about how you can approach your extraordinary life ahead.

With love and God bless,

Grace Andrews

P.S. If this devotional touches your heart after a week or two, I would be so grateful if you shared a brief review on Amazon. You're welcome to include a photo or video of your book if you like, though it's completely optional. Your review can help other Christians discover this devotional who might not find it otherwise. Thank you for sharing your love and supporting this work!

Starting Where You Are

God loves your mess exactly as it is

Week 1: Grateful for Fresh Starts

"Therefore, if anyone is in Christ, the new creation has come: The old has gone, the new is here!"

(2 CORINTHIANS 5:17)

Have you ever longed for a do-over? Maybe not a whole new year, but just a fresh Thursday afternoon. The dishwasher beeps, the day has slipped through your fingers, and all you want is to hit reset—or take a nap.

This longing for fresh starts runs deep in the human heart. You know the weight of regret. Words you wish you could take back. Choices you'd rather undo. Even prayers left unspoken because shame told you it was too late. Failure sits heavy, convincing you that this is all you'll ever be.

But God says something different. In Christ, you are not doomed to replay the same broken record. You are not just the sum of your yesterdays. Scripture declares: If anyone is in Christ, the new creation has come. The old has gone, the new is here.

Notice it doesn't say, "The old will eventually go when you've cleaned yourself up." It says it is already gone. You don't always feel new. Your habits still cling. Your failures echo. But truth is not measured by your feelings. Truth rests in what God has done. In Christ, you are not patched up, you are remade.

Fresh starts rarely arrive with fireworks. More often they slip in through ordinary obedience, like apologizing first, showing up again, or praying when words feel thin. God's mercy is steady, not sudden, and most new beginnings are built one surrendered moment at a time.

A fresh start in Him does not erase the past, but it breaks the power of the past to define you. What once held you captive no longer names you. Your story does not end in regret. It unfolds in redemption.

So when the heaviness creeps in and whispers that you'll never change, answer with God's word: the old has gone, the new is here. Even this ordinary day—this tired afternoon—is holy ground because the Creator has called you new.

You don't have to feel ready.

You don't have to deserve it.

You simply receive what Christ has already secured for you.

This Week's Prayer

*Lord, You know how quickly I slip into believing my past defines me.
The weight of regret feels stronger than the hope of change.
But Your word says I am a new creation in Christ.*

*The old has gone, and the new has already come.
Help me trust that promise when my feelings disagree.*

*Teach me to step into the freedom You've given me,
not because I am strong but because You are faithful.*

*Thank You for fresh starts that flow from Your grace,
not my effort. Amen.*

Where do you need a fresh start today? Be honest about where God is inviting you to begin again.

How would it change your gratitude if you saw each new beginning not as something you earned, but as a gift of mercy?

Looking back, where has God surprised you with fresh starts before? What does that remind you about His faithfulness now?

Week 2: Meeting Me in My Mess

"...to bestow on them a crown of beauty instead of ashes, the oil of joy instead of mourning, and a garment of praise instead of a spirit of despair."

(ISAIAH 61:3)

Have you ever looked around and thought, this is a mess?

Not the kind a quick wipe will fix, but the kind that seems to have seeped into everything.

You wake to find the remains of last night's meal still waiting because you were too tired to finish cleaning. And now, somehow, you feel even more tired facing it in the light of morning. On the fridge, a note nags at you about a bill you've been avoiding.

And then that heavy feeling creeps in—you don't even know where to start.

Ashes take different forms. Sometimes they're the remains of a conversation that left more hurt than healing. Sometimes they're the silence after praying for something that never came. Sometimes they're the dull ache of living the same weary rhythm day after day. You tell yourself you should be more grateful, more disciplined, more together. You promise God you'll come close again once you've managed to clean things up.

But God's promise through Isaiah interrupts that cycle. He first spoke it to people weighed down by exile, grieving what they had lost, wondering if they would ever see joy again. And His words still echo now. Beauty doesn't wait for everything to sparkle. God brings it right into the middle of the ashes. And joy? It slips in even when you're too worn out to go looking for it.

This is the strange hope of gratitude—it grows right in the middle of the mess. It's not that you pretend things are fine, but because you dare to believe that God hasn't left. He isn't waiting for you to scrub yourself clean. He isn't holding back until your prayers sound eloquent. Even the places you'd rather keep hidden are places He enters with healing.

Today may not bring sweeping change. It might be as small as noticing one mercy: the way your breathing slowed when you thought it never would. Or the verse you stumbled across that seemed written just for you. Those moments don't erase the ashes, but they remind you that God is already here, already working.

Your mess doesn't scare Him. It never has.

This Week's Prayer

Lord, I bring You what feels unfixable. I keep thinking I have to tidy myself before I draw near, but You promise beauty where there are ashes and joy where mourning still lingers. Meet me in the middle of what I can't control. Help me trust that You're not waiting for me to be better before You love me.

Teach me to notice the small mercies that show You're already here. Take the heaviness I carry and turn it into praise that rises from grace alone.

Amen.

What "ashes" in your life feel most difficult to bring before God, and how might opening that place to Him shift the way you see His mercy at work?

How has waiting for your life to be "clean enough" for authentic worship or gratitude actually kept you from experiencing God's transforming presence in your everyday chaos?

When you look back on the times in your life that felt like a mess, what signs of God's presence or restoring work can you see now, and how can remembering those moments grow your trust today?

Week 3: Caffeinated Morning Prayers

"Let the morning bring me word of your unfailing love, for I have put my trust in you. Show me the way I should go, for to you I entrust my life."

(PSALM 143:8)

Mornings have a way of exposing you. The alarm buzzes too soon, and before you've even had your first sip of coffee, the day is already pressing at the edges. You're awake, technically. But your soul? It still feels like it's hitting snooze. You scroll, you sigh, you stall—and still the morning waits for you.

David knew what it was to face mornings heavy with need. When he wrote Psalm 143, he wasn't living an easy life. His enemies surrounded him, his strength was fading, and he had more questions than answers. Yet his cry was simple: Let the morning bring me word of your unfailing love.

Notice what he doesn't ask for first. Not rescue. Not a checklist for success. He pleads for one thing before anything else—assurance of God's love. Because when you know you are loved, you can keep walking, even when the path is unclear.

Mornings carry a kind of mercy all their own. Yesterday's failures may still feel fresh to you, but the sunrise whispers that they don't get the last word. Each new day is another reminder that God's love is steady and that His compassions have not run out.

You are starting this day held, not condemned.

Your mornings may not be filled with literal enemies, but they can still feel like battlefields. Some mornings, weariness about the day ahead seeps in before you've even started. The coffee drips slower than usual, and you're already wondering if you've got what it takes to face another round of ordinary demands.

This is where prayer becomes more than a ritual. It becomes breath. Sometimes only one word makes it out: Help. Other times, silence does the talking. Either way, God hears. And just as David trusted God to guide his steps, you too can entrust your ordinary mornings to Him.

You don't need to start the day perfectly. You only need to start honestly.

Bring your tired eyes. Place the half-empty mug on the table. Let the clutter in your mind spill into His hands. Gratitude begins right there, not after the caffeine kicks in, but when you realize God's love has already arrived with the morning.

This Week's Prayer

God, thank You for mornings that come with Your unfailing love, even when I'm barely conscious enough to receive it. When my mind races ahead to everything I need to accomplish, help me pause long enough to entrust my plans to You. If worry tries to hijack my morning, remind me that Your love arrives fresh each day, more reliable than my coffee maker and more necessary than caffeine. Help me find You in the quiet moments before the day demands my attention. Show me the way I should go today.

Amen.

When you think of your mornings, what usually shapes your first thoughts—worry, weariness, or worship—and how might starting with prayer shift that pattern?

What specific aspects of your morning—whether it's your first cup of coffee, the quiet before others wake up, or even the rush to get ready—can become opportunities to practice thankfulness for God's daily provision and presence?

How does David's cry for God's love before anything else reshape the way you think about your own priorities at the start of each day?

Week 4: When Gratitude Feels Fake

"How long, Lord? Will you forget me forever? How long will you hide your face from me? How long must I wrestle with my thoughts and day after day have sorrow in my heart?"

(PSALM 13:1-2)

Gratitude isn't always easy. Sometimes it feels forced, like repeating lines you don't believe. You want to feel thankful, but the words don't land. They fall flat, leaving you empty.

Someone tells you to "count your blessings," and you nod politely. But when you actually sit down with pen in hand, ready to make a gratitude list, the page stays blank. The blessings you know exist feel far away, and all you can name is the silence. Instead of thankful, you feel like a fraud.

David knew that feeling. Look at Psalm 13. He doesn't open with thanksgiving. He doesn't list three good things. He cries out, How long, Lord? How long will You let me feel forgotten? You can feel his raw desperation when you read that passage.

This is the gift of David's honesty. It shows you that God doesn't demand pretend gratitude. He invites you to bring the truth of how you feel, even when it's anger, confusion, or sorrow. Gratitude that matters isn't forced. It can't be. Instead, it grows out of trust, and trust begins with honesty.

Maybe you've been told that real Christians never complain, that faith means putting on a smile and finding the silver lining. But Scripture tells a different story. God saw fit to include David's questions, complaints, and accusations in the very book that shapes our prayers. If He can handle David's anger and despair, He can handle yours too.

Sit with that for a moment. The same God who created galaxies gave space in His Word for human voices cracking under the weight of sorrow.

He isn't offended when your gratitude feels broken. He doesn't walk away when all you bring is complaint. Instead, He meets you there.

And notice this: David's lament didn't end in despair. By the end of Psalm 13, he remembered God's unfailing love. But he didn't skip straight there. He walked through the pain, named it, and only then did his heart turn toward hope.

That's the path to authentic gratitude. It doesn't mean denying your feelings. Instead, bring them fully into God's presence. Sometimes the most grateful thing you can do is admit you're not grateful at all, and trust that God will meet you in that honesty.

So if your prayer today sounds more like complaint than thanksgiving, know this—it counts. God sees it as faith, not failure.

This Week's Prayer

God, I'm tired of pretending I feel grateful when I don't. Thank You for David's example that shows me I can bring my real emotions to You, even when they're messy or angry. You're not scared of my questions or disappointed by my doubt.

Help me trust that wrestling with You leads to real gratitude, the deep kind that comes from discovering You can handle my emotions and love me anyway. Amen.

When gratitude feels forced or fake, what would it look like for you to bring honesty to God instead of a polished list of blessings?

How does Psalm 13 challenge the idea that faith means hiding your struggles, and how might David's honesty give you permission to pray more openly?

How might avoiding hard emotions keep you from true gratitude, and what could change if you, like David, brought your complaints to God before seeking thankfulness?

Week 5: Grateful for Permission to Not Be Okay

"Record my misery; list my tears on your scroll— are they not in your record?"

(PSALM 56:8)

Have you ever felt pressure to keep it all together? To smile in public when your insides feel like they're collapsing? Sometimes the hardest part of faith isn't believing in God's power. It is believing He welcomes you when you're not okay.

David made an audacious request in this psalm. He asked God to keep track of his suffering, not his victories or spiritual triumphs, but his misery and his tears. To David, pain mattered enough to be remembered forever. What kind of God does that? The kind who loves you completely, including the parts of your life that aren't polished or presentable. The God who sees worth in every tear you've cried and calls them precious enough to record.

That means you don't have to paste on a grin or rush into praise when your heart is heavy. Gratitude doesn't mean pretending. It means acknowledging that God is present even in the breaking. Sometimes the most faithful prayer is simply: This hurts.

Maybe you've been told to be strong or to count your blessings when life was falling apart. Those words can land like extra weight. But God doesn't shame you for weakness. He doesn't scold you for crying. Instead, He leans close, gathering every tear, and holding them as precious.

This is where gratitude becomes something so much deeper than a performance. It is not about writing down blessings to impress others or forcing words that sound right in a Bible study circle. It is about dragging your raw, unfiltered ache into God's presence and daring to believe He will not turn away. That kind of gratitude is not shallow; it is costly. It grows from wrestling and long nights soaked with tears, from the honest confession that you cannot fix yourself.

Gratitude grows differently in these moments. It is not loud or polished. It is quiet, almost fragile. It whispers a simple thank You: You see me, even here. This kind of gratitude doesn't erase the pain, but it is the one thing that keeps your heart fixed on the reality of His presence.

Here is the paradox. When you stop pretending to be okay, honesty makes room for comfort. Even tears can become a doorway to God's presence.

So if today finds you crying, weary, or worn down, let that be your offering. Your tears are known and written, cherished by the One who loves you.

This Week's Prayer

God, thank You for loving me in my struggle, not waiting until I get my act together. Thank You that my tears matter enough to You to be recorded, that my hardest days don't disqualify me from Your love. Thank You that You keep record of every sorrow I carry, as well as my joy. Give me the courage to bring my weakness to You without shame. Teach me to find gratitude not in denying my pain but in knowing You are near, collecting every tear. Hold me in my not-okayness and hold me steady.
Amen.

Where do you feel pressure to "be okay," and how might bringing that struggle honestly to God shift your perspective?

How does the image of God recording your tears change the way you think about His nearness in moments of pain?

What might it look like to practice gratitude today, not by denying your hurt, but by thanking God that He sees and values even your tears?

Week 6: Thank You for Ordinary Days

*"Give thanks in all circumstances;
for this is God's will for you in Christ Jesus."*

(1 THESSALONIANS 5:18)

Some days pass without leaving much of a mark. The sky looks the same as yesterday. Your evening feels routine. Dinner is reheated leftovers. Nothing is wrong, but nothing feels remarkable either. These are the kinds of days you rarely post about or even remember.

Yet Paul's command in 1 Thessalonians 5:18 presses right into these kinds of moments: Give thanks in all circumstances. Not just when prayers are answered or blessings overflow. All circumstances, even the ones that feel painfully ordinary.

This doesn't mean pretending every detail of your day is exciting. It means noticing that the ordinary is still threaded with grace. A quiet conversation that steadies you. The way your body still carries you when you're tired. Or even the light slipping through a window you've stopped noticing. These don't shout, but they whisper of God's presence.

Ordinary days matter because they're where most of your life is actually lived. And if gratitude can take root there, in the overlooked details and in the pauses that don't get remembered, it won't be easily shaken when the storms come.

Paul's words weren't written to people living glamorous lives. They were ordinary believers, working their jobs, raising families, facing struggles that looked painfully normal. His call to gratitude wasn't about chasing constant spiritual highs. It was about finding God in the daily grind, trusting that His presence made even routine faithfulness holy. The quiet choices, the hidden prayers, the unnoticed kindnesses—these matter deeply to Him.

Maybe you've been waiting for a breakthrough. Maybe you've been wishing something, anything, would break the routine. God sees that longing. But He also offers Himself right here, in the unremarkable hours that feel like filler. These are not wasted days. They are spaces where God's faithfulness shows up in quiet, sustaining ways.

Gratitude in ordinary days is less about feeling inspired and more about paying attention. It's saying, God, thank You that You're still here. Thank You that today is held in Your hands, even if it looks like yesterday.

And perhaps this is why Paul could tell weary believers to give thanks in all things. Gratitude isn't chained to circumstances. It flows from knowing that every circumstance, ordinary or extraordinary, is already held in Christ.

This Week's Prayer

Lord, thank You for days that don't stand out. The ones that feel small, repetitive, or forgettable. Remind me that these hours are not wasted but woven with Your presence. Help me to see Your gifts in the ordinary: the breath in my lungs, the steady beat of my heart, the people I cross paths with without thinking twice. Teach me to be grateful not just for the mountaintop moments but for the everyday mercies that carry me. Meet me here, in the quiet of the ordinary.
Amen.

What aspects of your most ordinary, routine day can you identify as evidence of God's faithful provision, and how might expressing gratitude for these "small" things change your perspective on mundane moments?

How does practicing gratitude in the midst of ordinary circumstances prepare your heart to remain thankful when bigger challenges or blessings arrive?

In what ways can you remind yourself that God's presence is just as real in the unremarkable days as in the extraordinary ones?

Week 7: Finding God in the Daily Grind

"And whatever you do, whether in word or deed, do it all in the name of the Lord Jesus, giving thanks to God the Father through him."

(COLOSSIANS 3:17)

The grind sneaks up on you. The alarm goes off, you reach for your phone, and the cycle begins again. Same commute. Same inbox. Same unmade bed in the morning. You tell yourself you'll get ahead, but most days it feels like you're just running in place.

It's easy to believe God only shows up in the big moments—the breakthroughs, the answers, the miracles you receive from Him. But Colossians 3:17 pushes against that: And whatever you do, whether in word or deed, do it all in the name of the Lord Jesus, giving thanks to God the Father through him. Paul wrote these words to ordinary believers, not spiritual celebrities. They were people who worked fields, raised children, cooked meals, and struggled to live out their faith in everyday life. Gratitude wasn't reserved for their mountaintop experiences. It was meant for the grind.

The daily grind isn't wasted space. It's the soil where character grows, where faithfulness takes root, where love gets practiced in hidden ways. The patience you show in traffic. The effort you pour into tasks no one thanks you for. The quiet decision to forgive instead of snap. Even folding laundry or answering another round of emails—these small things can become offerings when done in His name.

And yet the grind can feel soul-draining. The noise of deadlines, the cycle of chores, the endless repetition can wear you thin. You wonder if God notices, if He cares about the parts of life no one else applauds. But Scripture says He does. Nothing is beneath His notice, not even the smallest act done with Him in mind.

That's why gratitude matters here. It's not about forcing yourself to love the grind. It's about pausing long enough to remember that God is present in it. He stands with you in the cubicle, in the kitchen, even in the car. Every repetitive task can become an act of worship when you invite Him into it.

Maybe today isn't a mountaintop day. Maybe it's just another round of the same tasks. But even in the repetition, you can whisper thanks. It isn't because the grind feels glorious, but because God is with you in it. His presence makes even ordinary labor holy.

Gratitude in the grind doesn't mean loving every moment. It means refusing to believe any moment is godless.

This Week's Prayer

Lord, the repetition wears me down.
The work feels endless, and I wonder if it matters.

Does it?

Thank You that You see what no one else notices. Thank You that even the hidden work of my hands matters to You. Teach me to find Your presence in the middle of what feels small and unimportant. Give me eyes to see Your grace in the grind, and strength to keep going when I feel like giving up.

Let my labor be an offering of love.

Amen.

Where does your daily grind feel most discouraging, and how might gratitude shift the way you approach it?

How does Colossians 3:17 reshape the way you see your ordinary work, even when it feels unnoticed?

What is one small way you could practice gratitude in the middle of today's routine tasks?

Week 8: Grateful AND Grieving

"...sorrowful, yet always rejoicing; poor, yet making many rich; having nothing, and yet possessing everything."

(2 CORINTHIANS 6:10)

Grief strips the world of its color.

Food tastes flat. Music hurts. Time crawls, but somehow the days still vanish.

And in the middle of that ache, someone says, "Be grateful." The words hit like a slap.

Paul doesn't shy away from that tension. He says in 2 Corinthians 6:10 that he is "sorrowful, yet always rejoicing." Not one after the other. Both at once. He shows you that gratitude doesn't erase grief, and grief doesn't cancel gratitude. They can live side by side.

And that coexistence is messy. You thank God for one thing while the tears fall for another. A memory makes you laugh, then steals your breath. And you smile through gritted teeth in public, only to hit the floor when the room is empty. None of that makes you less faithful. It makes you human. Faith isn't the absence of contradiction, it's the courage to bring the contradiction into God's presence.

Grief does not disqualify you from thankfulness. And thankfulness doesn't mean your grief has disappeared. They can sit together in your chest, heavy and holy. One moment you whisper, Thank You for the years we had. The next, you can barely breathe because of the loss. Both are real. Both belong in God's presence.

Maybe you're grieving an empty chair at the table. Or the silence of a phone that doesn't ring anymore. Maybe it's not death but disappointment—the dream that fell apart, the relationship that broke, the future that looks nothing like what you prayed for. Gratitude doesn't mean denying those wounds. It means daring to bring them, exactly as they are, into God's hands.

Sometimes gratitude in grief sounds like defiance: I still believe You are good, even as I break apart. Sometimes it's softer: Thank You for holding me when I can't hold myself. And sometimes it's wordless—just tears slipping down, prayers too deep for language.

This is the mystery of faith. That joy and sorrow can share the same space. That hope can still breathe in the midst of mourning. That gratitude can endure, not by pretending the grief is gone, but because God refuses to leave.

Grateful and grieving. Both true. Both allowed. And in that fragile space, God meets you with a love big enough to hold both.

This Week's Prayer

Lord, I am grieving, and I don't want to pretend otherwise. The ache feels bigger than my strength, and the emptiness shadows every part of my day. Does it matter that I still feel this broken?

Thank You that You don't turn away from my sorrow. Thank You that my tears matter to You. Teach me to bring gratitude into this space without faking joy I don't feel. Show me how to trust Your goodness when all I see is loss. Hold me together when I can't hold myself.

Amen.

What loss or disappointment are you currently grieving that you've felt pressure to "get over" in order to be more grateful, and how might giving yourself permission to feel both emotions change your healing process?

How does Paul's phrase "sorrowful, yet always rejoicing" challenge your understanding of gratitude?

Where have you seen glimpses of God's presence in your grief, even in the smallest ways?

Week 9: Thank You for Crying With Me

"For we do not have a high priest who is unable to empathize with our weaknesses, but we have one who has been tempted in every way, just as we are—yet he did not sin."

(HEBREWS 4:15)

Tears can make you feel exposed. You wipe them away fast, as if crying proves you're weak. You say sorry for breaking down, wondering if God expects you to hold it together better than this.

But Hebrews 4:15 reminds you: Jesus doesn't watch from a distance with polite sympathy; He enters into your pain because He has lived it Himself.

At Lazarus's tomb, He did more than comfort grieving sisters. He wept with them. Even knowing He could raise Lazarus in minutes, He allowed His grief to show, demonstrating that love often expresses itself through tears.

Maybe you've felt the need to apologize to God for not being stronger, trusting more, or controlling your emotions. Perhaps you've wondered if your tears show weak faith. Here's what changes everything: Jesus has felt what you're feeling.

You've probably felt the sting of shallow comfort, the advice, the clichés, the push to 'move on.' Then there was the one who sat beside you with tissues in hand, saying nothing. That silence said everything. Presence mattered more than words, and that is what Jesus does.

He knows what it's like when friends drift away instead of staying with you. He knows the sting when people turn their backs, and the ache of praying in agony and hearing nothing back. None of this is foreign to Him.

And He cried. Not in private. Not hidden. In front of everyone. The Son of God with tears running down His face. If He didn't hide His pain, why do you feel like you have to hide yours?

Here's the truth. Gratitude can grow right in the middle of tears. Not because the ache disappears, but because you are not abandoned in it. You have a Savior who doesn't brush off your sorrow but joins you in it.

So when the weight presses down, don't hold back. Your tears are not a failure of faith. They're proof of your humanity. Proof that you feel. Proof that you need Him.

Gratitude doesn't mean pretending the hurt is gone. It means daring to believe your tears are seen, shared, and sacred in His presence.

This Week's Prayer

Jesus, thank You for choosing to experience human pain so You could understand mine. Thank You for not standing at a distance from my sorrow but stepping into it.

My heart feels raw, my body heavy, and I still feel empty. Sit with me here.

When others tell me to move on, remind me that You stayed at the tomb long enough to weep. Teach me to bring my tears without shame, to let gratitude rise not from denial but from Your nearness.

Hold me steady when I can't hold myself.

Amen.

When have you felt pressure to hide your tears, and how does Jesus' empathy change the way you see them?

How does the image of Jesus weeping at Lazarus's tomb help you understand His heart for your pain?

When you focus on gratitude for a God who "cries with you" rather than just "fixes your problems," what does this reveal about the kind of relationship He desires with you, and how does thankfulness for His understanding change your perspective on suffering?

Week 10: Coffee Cup Communion

"You prepare a table before me in the presence of my enemies. You anoint my head with oil; my cup overflows."

(PSALM 23:5)

Steam rises from your morning mug, wrapping the air with comfort before the day has even begun. In that simple ritual, God sometimes speaks the loudest, through warmth, aroma, and the reminder that you are already cared for.

David pictured a God who turns scarcity into plenty. Tables prepared with care invited presence and blessing. Rich oil anointed and honored beyond necessity. Cups spilled over, brimming with abundance for all who came.

This paints a picture of a God who delights in giving good gifts that go beyond mere survival.

Maybe this morning the sunrise surprised you with your favorite colors, or your favorite song came on the radio at the perfect moment. Perhaps someone brought donuts to work for no special reason, or you discovered a forgotten twenty-dollar bill in your coat pocket. These aren't life-changing moments, but they're life-brightening ones—small luxuries that feel like love notes from heaven.

Our culture often makes us feel guilty for enjoying anything that isn't strictly necessary. We're told to be grateful for what we have while secretly feeling selfish for wanting more than basic sustenance. But David's psalm suggests that God actually enjoys providing luxuries, not because we've earned them, but because love expresses itself through generosity.

When you're grateful for small luxuries, you're acknowledging that God's care extends beyond meeting your minimum requirements. He created sunsets when streetlights would suffice, gave strawberries their sweetness when nutrition could be flavorless, and designed laughter to be contagious when communication could be purely functional.

David found himself surrounded by enemies, yet he could still celebrate the overflowing cup, the prepared table, and the anointing oil. Even in difficult circumstances, God's goodness showed up in ways that brought comfort and joy beyond what survival required. When we practice gratitude for small luxuries, we're training our hearts to recognize God's presence in pleasure, not just in provision.

This doesn't make us materialistic or entitled. Instead, it develops our capacity to receive love in its many forms, building resilience for harder days by creating a reservoir of remembered kindness.

Your overflowing cup today becomes strength for tomorrow's drought.

This Week's Prayer

God, I don't need much this morning, just enough strength to get through the day. Yet You give me more. Sometimes it feels silly that a cup of coffee can feel holy, but here I am—savoring the warmth, breathing in the steam, and finding You in the ordinary.
Thank You for caring about my joy, not just my survival.

When guilt tells me I don't deserve this abundance, remind me that You love to overflow cups. Help me taste Your kindness in small pleasures and carry that gratitude into the harder hours of my day.
Amen.

What small luxuries or simple pleasures have you been dismissing as unimportant rather than recognizing them as expressions of God's kindness, and how might gratitude for these "extras" change your daily awareness of His care?

How has feeling guilty about enjoying non-essential pleasures affected your ability to receive God's generosity, and what would it look like to embrace His desire to bring you joy through small gifts?

When you think about God preparing a table and providing an overflowing cup even in difficult circumstances, what current small luxuries in your life can you thank Him for, regardless of what challenges you're facing?

Week 11: Grateful for Friends Who Get It

"Though one may be overpowered, two can defend themselves. A cord of three strands is not quickly broken."

(ECCLESIASTES 4:12)

There's a quiet relief in being understood.

Not the polite nod someone gives when they're trying to keep up, but the kind of recognition that makes you feel seen without explanation. You don't have to defend yourself or reshape your words so they'll land softer. You just speak, and they already know.

The writer of Ecclesiastes once said that two are stronger than one, and he wasn't exaggerating. Loneliness wears people down. A single person facing the storm is often crushed. Add a companion and suddenly the fight doesn't feel as impossible. Bring God into the middle of it, and the bond isn't just strong. It is the kind that resists breaking even when life pulls hard.

Maybe you've got someone like that.

The friend who hears the tremor in your voice before you've admitted you're scared. The one who doesn't offer quick fixes or lecture you to be tougher. They show up, sit with you, and make the room feel lighter just by being there.

When someone shows up for you in that way, it is more than human kindness. It is a glimpse of God's own heart. He designed friendship to echo His presence, reminding you that you are not meant to carry burdens by yourself. Their care becomes living proof that He hears your cries and sends help through the people who love you.

The image of a cord woven three ways isn't just poetry. It is survival. Friendships without depth are fragile. They unravel when distance grows or disagreements surface. But relationships with God at their center don't snap so easily. They bend. They stretch. And they last.

Being grateful for friends who get it means recognizing these relationships as gifts, not guarantees. They pull you forward when you've stopped believing in yourself. Not everyone will understand you, but when someone does and they see past your defenses to your heart, that is worth celebrating.

And if you don't have that person yet, don't lose hope. Keep your eyes open, but more importantly, keep becoming the kind of friend you wish you had.

Chances are, someone else is praying for the very kind of presence you're learning to give. When God weaves those cords together, gratitude becomes the strongest strand of all.

This Week's Prayer

Lord, sometimes I feel alone, even in a crowd.

Thank You for the rare gift of friends who see me and don't need me to explain. Their presence feels like shelter when I'm worn out and scared.

Remind me not to take them for granted.

And when the loneliness feels louder than their nearness, hold me close and be the Friend who never leaves. Teach me to love others with that same faithfulness.

Amen.

Who has stood with you in a way that made life's challenges feel less overwhelming, and how can you thank them—or thank God—for being His presence to you in those battles?

How has experiencing the strength of friendships woven together with God as the "third strand" changed your perspective on what you can face, and what about these bonds fills you with the most gratitude?

When you think about friends who truly "get it," what moments of understanding or acts of support come to mind, and how can thanking God for them today also deepen your connection with those friends?

Week 12: When Life Doesn't Match Expectations

"Many are the plans in a person's heart, but it is the Lord's purpose that prevails."

(PROVERBS 19:21)

What did you picture your life would look like by now? Most of us carry a mental snapshot of a marriage, a career, a family, a dream. And when reality doesn't match, it can feel like something has gone wrong.

Solomon knew something about plans gone sideways. Here was a man with unlimited resources, unmatched wisdom, and divine favor, yet even he had to admit that human planning has its limits. The wisest king who ever lived confessed that our expectations often collide with God's larger purposes.

And His purposes always win.

Maybe your life looks nothing like you thought it would. The career didn't unfold as planned. The relationship ended differently than expected. The family you dreamed of never came. Perhaps you're in a city you never meant to call home or working a job that pays the bills but doesn't fulfill your soul. Sometimes it feels like you're living someone else's life.

There's grief in unmet expectations. Real sorrow when dreams die or morph into something unrecognizable. The disappointment is valid, the sense of loss genuine. Naming the grief is part of gratitude, because it takes honesty to thank God in a place you never wanted to be. But buried within these crashed plans lies an invitation to gratitude deeper than anything our expectations could have produced.

When God's purpose prevails, it's not out of a desire to disappoint us. It's because His view spans eternity while ours barely covers next week. What looks like a detour from our perspective might be the main road from His.

Being grateful when life doesn't match expectations isn't about pretending you're not disappointed. It's about trusting that the God who sees the whole story is writing something beautiful even when you can only read the confusing middle chapters.

Maybe the job loss led to the career you never knew you wanted. The ended relationship cleared space for the person who truly values you. Sometimes what feels like failure becomes the foundation for something you couldn't have imagined.

This doesn't erase the pain of shattered expectations. But it does remind us that God's purposes often include plot twists that serve our good and His glory in ways our planning couldn't anticipate.

Your crashed expectations might just be the best thing that never happened to you.

This Week's Prayer

Lord, my life doesn't look the way I thought it would. Some dreams are gone, some doors have slammed shut, and it hurts more than I want to admit. Yet I trust that You see what I cannot. Thank You that Your purposes are bigger than my plans. Give me courage to lay down what I pictured so I can receive what You are actually giving. Teach me to be grateful, not because it's easy, but because You are faithful.

Amen.

What major unmet expectation in your life has led to unexpected blessings or growth you can now be grateful for, even though the original disappointment was real and painful?

How has seeing God's purposes prevail over your plans taught you to trust His character in new ways, and what aspects of His faithfulness through those redirections can you thank Him for today?

When you compare the life you're living with the life you once planned, what surprising gifts or opportunities has this different path provided, and how could gratitude for these shape your perspective on current disappointments?

Week 13: Thank You for Small Mercies

"Because of the Lord's great love we are not consumed, for his compassions never fail. They are new every morning; great is your faithfulness."

(LAMENTATIONS 3:22-23)

Jeremiah wrote these words from the ashes of Jerusalem. The city lay in ruins, the temple destroyed, and his people had scattered into exile. Everything he knew and loved had been stripped away. Yet, in the middle of this devastation, he found reason to speak of God's faithfulness. It wasn't that his circumstances had improved, but because he noticed something remarkable.

He was still breathing.

"We are not consumed." In other words, the worst thing that could happen didn't completely destroy us. There's still something left. Still air in our lungs, thoughts in our minds, and the capacity to notice that morning came again despite yesterday's disasters.

Maybe you're reading this from your own version of ruins. The day your life cracked wide open, and the future you imagined slipped through your hands. Or maybe it's something less dramatic but equally devastating—the slow erosion of a dream you can't quite let go of yet.

This is when small mercies become lifelines.

It could be that you slept a few uninterrupted hours when insomnia usually claims the whole night. Maybe it was the way your coffee tasted this morning when nothing else brings you comfort, or perhaps it was how a stranger held the door open when you felt invisible to the world. Jeremiah understood that God's compassions come in daily doses, not just dramatic deliverances. His faithfulness shows up in the small kindnesses that keep us from being completely consumed by whatever is trying to destroy us. These mercies don't fix everything, but they remind us that Love is still at work.

Small mercies don't arrive with fanfare. They slip in quietly through the cracks of our broken days, carrying just enough light to help us take the next step.

Your gratitude practice during hard times needs to start smaller than you thought. Instead of waiting to be thankful for life-changing breakthroughs, you can thank God for life-sustaining moments. The breath you just took. The bed that gave you rest.

None of this is second-best. It's God, steady and present, keeping you from being consumed when everything else has collapsed.

And that's something.

This Week's Prayer

*God, some days the weight feels too much and I wonder
if I'll make it through.*

Yet here I am, still breathing.

*Thank You for keeping me when I don't have the strength to keep myself.
When I feel like I'm at the edge of being consumed, pull me back with
Your mercy. Remind me that Your love is steady, even in ruins,
and that You will not let me be destroyed.*

Amen.

What small mercy or unexpected kindness carried you through a hard time, and how did seeing it as God's compassion change the way you endured?

When you hear the phrase "we are not consumed," what specific ways has God's faithfulness kept you going, and how can you thank Him for that today?

How might learning to notice and thank God for daily small mercies strengthen your faith for future struggles and help you sense His presence even without big breakthroughs?

Growing in Grace

Biblical wisdom that fits your daily life

Week 14: Grateful for Growth That Hurts

"Consider it pure joy, my brothers and sisters, whenever you face trials of many kinds, because you know that the testing of your faith produces perseverance."

(JAMES 1:2-3)

Let's be honest. Trials don't feel like joy. They feel like exhaustion, disorientation, and the slow unraveling of everything you thought you could handle. James didn't deny that. What he offered was a different lens: what hurts might also be shaping you in ways comfort never could.

The kind of growth that changes us rarely feels gentle. Muscles tear before they strengthen. Trees stand taller after storms. Metal only becomes pure when exposed to fire. And faith? Faith gets real when it's tested in ways we never would've chosen.

Maybe you're right there. In the middle of growth that stings. Not the soft kind you'd sign up for in a workshop, but the gritty kind that strips away illusions and forces you to face what's actually true. The situation that pushes past your usual coping strategies, exposing the parts of you that still need healing.

It's disorienting. And exhausting.

James wasn't just speaking in theory. He'd seen what pressure does to people.

When he talks about joy in trials, he's not being insincere. He's not telling anyone to enjoy suffering. He's simply pointing to what it produces. A kind of perseverance that can't be faked. A faith that holds up when everything else collapses.

Gratitude in the middle of that doesn't mean liking the pain. It just means you're willing to admit that some of the most important parts of who you're becoming are being formed here, in the ache.

Perseverance isn't passive. It's not just gritting your teeth. It's something active that starts to take root in you. The spiritual reflexes that help you keep going when the bottom drops out. The ability to spot God's fingerprints in places you used to overlook.

And maybe, slowly, your pain starts doing something. It grows compassion in you. It sharpens your discernment. It clears space for something new to take root.

This doesn't minimize what hurts. But it does suggest that nothing is wasted.

Growth that hurts often produces a kind of strength you didn't know you had. The quiet confidence that even in your weakness, God is still strong.

And maybe, just maybe, that's worth holding on to.

This Week's Prayer

God, I don't like this. I don't like the ache, the pressure, or the waiting. But if this pain is shaping something in me that matters, don't let me waste it. Hold me together when I want to quit. Grow in me the kind of faith that doesn't crack under fire. Teach me to see You in the struggle, and to trust that nothing is wasted in Your hands.

Amen.

What painful experience has produced growth or maturity you can now thank God for, even though you wouldn't want to repeat the process?

How has recognizing God's presence during past trials shaped your ability to trust Him now, and what aspects of that perseverance can you thank Him for today?

In your current challenges, what changes in character, priorities, or faith can you already see forming that wouldn't have developed otherwise

Week 15: Thank You for Unanswered Prayers

"Three times I pleaded with the Lord to take it away from me. But he said to me, 'My grace is sufficient for you, for my power is made perfect in weakness.'"

(2 CORINTHIANS 12:8-9)

You've prayed. Pleaded. Bargained. Waited. And still—silence. Few things cut as deep as God's "no" or "not yet." Paul knew that ache too. Even with miracles and visions behind him, when he begged God for relief, the answer was no because He had something better in mind.

Sometimes the prayers God doesn't answer protect us from getting what we want at the expense of what we need.

Maybe you've been praying for years about something that feels urgent and necessary to your happiness. You've asked, begged, bargained, and waited. Still, silence.

Paul's experience teaches us that unanswered prayers aren't evidence of God's absence or indifference. They're often evidence of His deeper love, the kind that sees beyond our immediate desires to our ultimate good.

What if the relationship you keep asking God to fix is the one He's protecting you from? What if the door He won't open is saving you from a path that would pull you away from His best? Even the healing He withholds can become space to discover His sufficiency in ways perfect health never could.

This doesn't mean every unanswered prayer is a blessing in disguise. But it does mean that His perspective spans eternity while ours barely covers next week.

Paul stopped fighting God's "no" and started receiving God's grace. Everything changed. His weakness became the platform for God's strength. The very thing he wanted removed became the source of his most powerful ministry.

Being grateful for unanswered prayers requires trust that goes against every instinct we have. It means believing that God's love is so deep He'll risk our temporary disappointment to ensure our eternal good.

Maybe your unanswered prayer is teaching you to find satisfaction in God Himself rather than in what He can do for you. Your current "no" from God might be protecting you from settling for less than His best. His silence might be an invitation to deepen your relationship with Him rather than just improving your circumstances.

That kind of surrender opens doors to blessings you never knew to ask for.

This Week's Prayer

God, unanswered prayers cut deep. I want relief, and when You say no, it hurts.

Yet I believe You see more than I can.

Thank You for protecting me even when I fight Your answer. Teach me to trust that Your grace is enough when nothing else is. When silence feels crushing, remind me You are near. Hold me steady in the ache, and give me peace in Your wisdom.

Amen.

What prayer God didn't answer the way you hoped has led to something better, and how has that deepened your gratitude for His wisdom in saying no?

How has learning to accept God's "no" or "not yet" changed your prayer life and relationship with Him, and what parts of that growth can you thank Him for today?

Looking at your current unanswered prayers, how might God's delay or denial be protecting you from less than His best, and how could gratitude shift your perspective in the waiting?

Week 16: Finding Joy in Being Known

"For now we see only a reflection as in a mirror; then we shall see face to face. Now I know in part; then I shall know fully, even as I am fully known."

(1 CORINTHIANS 13:12)

Mirrors only ever give you part of the truth. They show the angle you choose, the surface you allow. But God looks past the reflection. He notices the restless nights you try to laugh off. He sees the moments you regret and the ones you'd rather not name. He also sees the resilience that keeps you standing. And His love does not flinch.

He knows it all, and He loves us anyway.

Most of us spend a surprising amount of energy managing how others see us. We edit what we share, lean hard on strengths, soften or hide the parts we fear will cost us respect. Piece by piece, we construct portraits that feel safer than showing the real thing. It works for a while, but it's exhausting to keep holding the mask in place.

With God, that pressure disappears.

He already knows what you try to cover, even from yourself. He sees the restless thoughts, the jealous flashes, the selfish choices you'd rather forget. None of it shocks Him. None of it makes Him love you less.

There's something both terrifying and liberating about being completely known. Terrifying because we can't hide behind carefully constructed facades, yet liberating because we don't have to. The deepest human longing isn't just to be loved but to be known and still loved. To have someone see us completely and choose us anyway.

This is what God offers: rest from pretending and relief from the pressure to prove yourself. You don't have to earn His love, and you can't lose it when you fail. He sees you clearly in both your brokenness and your strength.

His commitment to you remains constant.

Being fully known by God doesn't mean you can use His acceptance as an excuse to stop growing. But it does mean you can approach Him without pretense. You can pray about your ugliest thoughts without shocking Him. You can confess your deepest failures without losing His love.

The mirror Paul mentions shows us reflections that are partial, sometimes distorted. Right now, your understanding of God is limited. But His understanding of you is complete, perfect, without distortion. One day you'll see Him as clearly as He sees you now. But today, you can rest in the joy of being fully seen by Him, and in the gratitude that His gaze is never harsh but always loving.

This Week's Prayer

God, You see all of me, and sometimes that thought scares me. I'd rather hide the messy parts, the doubts, the failures, the shadows I don't want to face. But You already know, and still You stay.

Thank You for loving me without conditions.

Teach me to rest in that love, to stop performing, to trust that being fully known by You is not a threat but a gift. Amen.

What aspects of yourself do you work hardest to hide from others, and how can you express gratitude for God's love that sees those parts clearly and never wavers because of them?

How has experiencing God's complete acceptance despite your flaws changed your understanding of love itself, and what specific ways can you thank Him for the freedom that comes from being fully known without fear of rejection?

When you think about God knowing your potential and not just your current struggles, what about His vision for your growth can you be genuinely grateful for, and how does His complete knowledge of who you're becoming encourage you today?

Week 17: Grateful for Second Chances

*"You will again have compassion on us;
you will tread our sins underfoot and hurl all
our iniquities into the depths of the sea."*

(MICAH 7:19)

Micah addressed people who had failed spectacularly. Israel had abandoned their covenant, chased other gods, ignored what God asked of them until judgment came and exile followed. By the standards of justice, they should have stayed there forever. Yet Micah insisted their story wasn't finished. God hadn't walked away.

The picture he paints is startling. God doesn't just forgive, He crushes sin under His feet like a defeated enemy and tosses it into the depths of the sea, gone for good. Not covered up. Not filed away. Obliterated.
Maybe you know what it feels like to need a second chance. It could be a relationship you've destroyed, poor decisions, or words you can't take back. You've stood in the wreckage of your own making, wondering if you'd used up all your chances for redemption.

Human forgiveness often runs out. We keep score, set limits, decide when enough is enough. But God doesn't count like we do. His mercy doesn't dry up after repeated failure. His love never hits a breaking point. When Micah describes God hurling sins into the sea, he's showing us forgiveness so complete that even God chooses not to bring them up again.

Being grateful for second chances means acknowledging that you didn't earn them and can't repay them. They're gifts from a God whose nature is to restore rather than discard. Every morning you wake up breathing is another chance to get it right.

These human second chances often mirror the divine one you've already received. God's willingness to give you another opportunity to love Him, serve Him, and live for His glory despite all the times you've chosen yourself instead.

Second chances don't erase consequences or guarantee that everything will return to exactly how it was before. But they do offer hope that failure doesn't have to be final, and that your worst moment doesn't determine your ultimate destiny.

When you're grateful for second chances, you're celebrating a God who specializes in resurrection. You're acknowledging that His love is stronger than your failure.

Your second chance might be happening right now as you read these words and realize that God hasn't given up on you yet. And neither should you.

This Week's Prayer

God, I've made mistakes I can't undo, and sometimes the shame still clings. Thank You that failure isn't the end with You.

Thank You for second chances I don't deserve and could never earn. Teach me to trust that when You forgive, it's gone for good. Help me stop dragging back what You've already hurled into the sea. Give me courage to begin again and grace to extend that same mercy to others.

Amen.

What second chance are you most grateful for, and how did receiving it change your understanding of God's grace?

How does knowing that God has hurled your sins "into the depths of the sea" affect your ability to forgive yourself today?

Who in your life needs a second chance from you, and how might gratitude for your own forgiveness help you extend that same mercy?

Week 18: Thank You for the God Who Sees

"She gave this name to the Lord who spoke to her: 'You are the God who sees me,' for she said, 'I have now seen the One who sees me.'"

(GENESIS 16:13)

Hagar was invisible to the people around her. A servant. A foreigner. A woman without status in Abraham's household. When conflict broke out with Sarah, she became disposable, pushed out into the wilderness with her son, and left to face whatever came next. No one with power seemed to care.

But there, desperate and thirsty, watching her child cry in the desert, she learned she wasn't invisible after all. God saw her. He knew her pain, spoke her name, and met her need with water. He even gave promises about her son's future, promises as weighty as the ones spoken over Isaac.

"You are the God who sees me," she said. El Roi. The God who notices. Not in some detached way, but with a gaze that is personal and close.

Maybe you've felt that kind of invisibility. Passed over for work you've done well. Talking and realizing no one is listening. Feeling forgotten by people who once promised to be there.

It leaves you wondering if anyone sees what you carry.

The truth Hagar found is still true now: you are seen by God. He notices the sleepless nights when bills keep you awake. He sees you holding back tears in public, doing work that gets no acknowledgment, and making sacrifices no one applauds. None of it slips past Him.

Gratitude for the God who sees means loosening your grip on the need for constant human recognition. Your worth doesn't rise or fall with applause, promotions, or how much others notice. You matter because you are His. That alone.

And He isn't only watching from a distance. He steps into the story. He nudges doors open you didn't even know were there, provides through unlikely sources, and stirs compassion in people who don't realize they're carrying His kindness to you.

Hagar's encounter didn't erase her struggles. She was still a single mother in a hard world. But she wasn't alone anymore. Neither are you. "You are the God who sees me." Let that truth settle deeper than disappointment.

You are not invisible. Not forgotten. Not ever.

This Week's Prayer

El Roi, sometimes I feel invisible.

My work goes unnoticed, my words fall flat, and I wonder if anyone truly sees me. But You do.

You see the weight I carry when no one else notices. You know the tears I hide, the sacrifices I make, the questions I'm afraid to ask out loud.

Thank You for seeing me when I feel forgotten and alone, and for reminding me I am never outside of Your care. When I ache for recognition, turn my heart back to You. Teach me to rest in Your gaze and to live secure in being fully seen and deeply loved by You. Amen.

When have you felt most invisible or overlooked by others, and what can you thank God for about His faithful attention during those times when human acknowledgment was absent?

What specific ways has God demonstrated that He sees your struggles, needs, or efforts, and how can expressing gratitude for these moments of divine recognition encourage you when others fail to notice?

How does being grateful for a God who sees you affect your need for human recognition and validation, and what does this teach you about finding your identity in His constant awareness rather than others' inconsistent attention?

Week 19: Celebrating Tiny Victories

*"Who dares despise the day of small things,
since the seven eyes of the Lord that range
throughout the earth will rejoice when they see
the chosen capstone in the hand of Zerubbabel?"*

(ZECHARIAH 4:10)

Tiny victories can feel insulting when you're desperate for a breakthrough. You wanted healing and got enough strength for a shower. You prayed for abundance and found only a crumpled bill in your pocket. It feels like not enough. But to God, it's worth celebrating.

Zechariah spoke to people rebuilding the temple after decades of exile. Their work looked pitiful compared to Solomon's original, and progress dragged on. Critics mocked. Even the builders doubted. But God saw it differently.

He celebrated every stone laid.

Tiny victories can feel insulting when the need is overwhelming. You pray for a financial breakthrough but find only a crumpled bill in your pocket. You want healing yet simply manage a shower. You long for a career shift but just get through the workday without breaking.

These moments seem small, but God notices. His eyes scan the earth, attentive to every act of faithfulness, each step of obedience, however quiet.

They may never impress anyone else, but they're shaping you. Every choice to keep going when quitting would be easier builds strength to carry weightier things later.

Jesus' parable of the talents shows God's economy. Faithful in little isn't preparation for more — it is the more. Reliability in small things is already success in His eyes.

Gratitude for tiny victories means learning to value progress made in inches, not miles. The person who sheds weight didn't do it overnight but in countless choices. The marriage that heals doesn't shift in one talk but through daily steps toward love.

Your tiny wins are proof of God's grace at work, even before the breakthrough. They testify that progress is happening, even if it looks nothing like what you envisioned.

These aren't consolation prizes. They are victories, honored by the God who sees everything.

Maybe the definition of victory needs to shrink to match His perspective. He celebrates progress, not perfection. Effort, not just results.

Don't despise the day of small things. God doesn't.

This Week's Prayer

God, I get frustrated when progress feels too small to matter. But You see every step, and You call it victory. Forgive me for despising small beginnings when You rejoice over them. Teach me to measure success by faithfulness, not by size. Thank You for the quiet miracles of grace that keep me moving when I want to give up.

Amen.

What tiny victory from this past week can you thank God for, even if it feels small compared to the bigger challenges you still face?

How has chasing only major breakthroughs kept you from gratitude in daily wins, and what might shift if you started celebrating small steps forward?

Where have you seen slow, steady growth over time, and how can you thank God for His faithfulness in those changes instead of wishing for instant transformation?

Week 20: Grateful for Grace in Relationships

"Bear with each other and forgive one another if any of you has a grievance against someone. Forgive as the Lord forgave you."

(COLOSSIANS 3:13)

Love sounds noble until it gets real. A careless word on the drive home. A silence that feels heavier than shouting. A wound that reopens just when you thought it was healed. That's where Paul's words land: "Bear with each other and forgive."

"Bear with each other" carries an assumption we would rather avoid: real relationships require endurance. Even the people you love most will let you down. They might wound you without meaning to, and sometimes they will hurt you even when they know it. And if you are honest, you have done the same. Rough edges show, bad moods spill out, and somebody ends up carrying more than their share.

Grace doesn't mean brushing it all aside or pretending it doesn't sting. It means staying engaged when retreating would feel easier. It means leaving space for someone to be fully human without excusing harm.

Sometimes that looks like listening more carefully. Other times it looks like silence because there is nothing left to say.

Paul roots forgiveness in God's own forgiveness, and that changes everything. You can bear with others because God bears with you. You can forgive what feels repetitive because you've been forgiven more times than you can count. Patience doesn't come from you. It comes from Him.

And gratitude shows up here too. Thank God for the ones who stay, who choose you even when you make it hard, and who forgive when you fall short. Thank Him also for giving you the ability to extend the same grace to others. Not because it is easy, but because His Spirit makes it possible.

Grace never means tolerating abuse. It doesn't erase boundaries or cancel accountability. But it shifts the posture of your heart. Sometimes it looks like having the same conversation yet again. Other times it is an apology you didn't want to make. Or a quiet decision to assume the best about someone's intent.

Difficult relationships aren't distractions from spiritual growth. They are the very place love is strengthened, tested, and stretched.

Every act of grace is a workout for the soul.

This Week's Prayer

God, relationships stretch me in ways I do not like at times. I want patience, but I run out of it fast. I want to forgive, but sometimes the hurt feels bigger than my capacity.

Thank You for not giving up on me when I am difficult, when I wound, when I fail. Help me not walk away too fast. Give me strength to stay when it is hard, to forgive when I would rather hold on, and to love out of Your grace instead of my limits.

Amen.

Who in your life has consistently extended grace to you when you've been difficult to love, and how can you express gratitude for their patience and forgiveness in specific ways?

What relationship in your life currently requires you to "bear with" someone, and what aspects of God's patient grace toward you can you thank Him for that might inspire more gracious responses in that challenging situation?

How has experiencing God's forgiveness for your own relational failures changed your ability to forgive others, and what can you thank Him for about the way He uses imperfect relationships to teach you deeper gratitude for His grace?

Week 21: Through, Not Around

*"When you pass through the waters, I will be with you;
and when you pass through the rivers,
they will not sweep over you."*

(ISAIAH 43:2)

God didn't promise to pave a smooth road across the floods or create a shortcut around the dangerous rivers. He promised something different: to walk through them with you. The assumption in Isaiah's words is clear. You will face waters that threaten to overwhelm you, rivers that seem impossible to cross.

But you won't face them alone.

This promise came to people heading into exile, who had lost everything they'd built, and faced an uncertain future far from home. God wasn't offering them an escape route from hardship but companionship through it. His presence would make the difference between drowning and surviving.

Maybe you've been asking God to remove you from difficult circumstances that seem to have no end in sight. You've wondered why He doesn't just fix everything instantly. Why does the path forward have to go through such challenging territory?

The truth hidden in Isaiah's promise is that some of life's most important transformations happen not by sidestepping our problems but by moving through them. The deepest trust in God's character develops in places where you can't see the way forward. Strong faith emerges from situations where you learn to depend completely on His guidance because your own resources aren't sufficient.

God walks with you through difficulty rather than around it, it's not that He's cruel or blind to your pain, but because His presence becomes real in ways that wouldn't be possible if He simply removed every obstacle. The mother sitting beside her child's hospital bed discovers God's comfort in ways she wouldn't have known if illness had never touched her family.

Being grateful for God's presence through hardship doesn't mean you have to be thankful for the hardship itself. You can grieve the loss of someone close to you while appreciating how God provides strength for each difficult minute of the day.

The waters and rivers Isaiah mentions aren't gentle streams. They're torrents strong enough to pull you under. Yet God's promise isn't that you'll avoid getting wet but that you won't be overwhelmed.

Your current struggle isn't evidence that God has abandoned you. It's the place where you can discover that His promise is true: the waters won't sweep over you because He's walking through them beside you. That presence in the depths of difficulty becomes strength that carries you long after the crisis has passed.

This Week's Prayer

God, thank You for staying with me in the hard places instead of clearing every obstacle out of the way. I confess I want the quick fix. I want the easy way. When You don't remove the pain, help me notice how You sit with me in it. Thank You that I don't have to face overwhelming waters on my own. Your promise to stay with me is steadier than any guarantee of comfort. Give me faith to trust Your presence even when I can't see the plan. Amen.

When have you sensed God's presence most clearly in a difficult time, and what about His companionship through it can you thank Him for today?

How has walking through challenges with God, rather than having Him remove them, reshaped your view of His love and faithfulness, and what gratitude does that stir in you now?

What current situation are you asking God to take you around instead of through, and how might thanking Him for His promise to stay with you shift the way you face it?

Week 22: Finding God in Waiting Rooms

*"Wait for the Lord; be strong and take heart
and wait for the Lord."*

(PSALM 27:14)

David knew what it was like to wait with his life hanging in the balance. Hunted by King Saul, hiding in caves, uncertain if he would survive another day, he understood that waiting isn't just about patience. It is about holding on to hope when you cannot see what comes next. His repetition of "wait for the Lord" wasn't redundant; it was like a rhythm that keeps your heart beating when everything else feels stopped.

Waiting rooms, especially in hospitals, are among the most honest places on earth. These are the spaces where pretense falls away and you are left with raw need, honest fear, and the question of whether God is present when life feels suspended.

Maybe you are in a waiting room right now, literal or metaphorical. Waiting for test results that could change everything or for a job offer that would solve your financial stress. The space between asking and receiving can feel like the loneliest place in the world.

But David discovered something powerful about waiting. It isn't empty time where nothing happens. It is sacred space where faith either grows stronger or reveals what it is really made of. His words "be strong and take heart" aren't casual encouragement but a description of what becomes possible when you wait *with* God rather than just waiting *for* God.

Being grateful in waiting requires a different kind of vision. Instead of focusing only on what you are waiting for, you can thank God for what you are discovering while you wait. The strength you didn't know you had facing uncertainty. The prayers you never thought you would pray. Messy. Desperate. Unfiltered. Your waiting might be teaching you to depend on God in ways prosperity never could.

Waiting strips away the illusion that you are in control. It forces you to face the reality that some of life's most important questions can only be answered by time and circumstances outside your influence. But it also becomes a classroom where you learn that God's presence doesn't depend on favorable outcomes.

The waiting you are in right now is not a punishment or a mistake. It is where God meets you in your vulnerability, and where anxiety can be reshaped into trust. David says it twice: wait for the Lord. Not passive resignation, but active trust.

This Week's Prayer

God, waiting wears me out.

I want answers now, not silence.

I want relief, not delay.

Thank You that even in the in-between, You have not left me.

When fear rises and time feels heavy, remind me that waiting with You is not wasted. Teach me to trust Your presence when I cannot see Your plan. Strengthen me to hold on when I would rather give up.

Thank You that You are near in the places that feel most uncertain.

Amen.

What waiting room experience—literal or metaphorical—has taught you the most about God's faithfulness, and what aspects of His presence during that time can you thank Him for today?

How has being forced to wait for something important changed your perspective on God's timing and control in ways that you can be genuinely grateful for, even if the waiting was difficult?

What are you currently waiting for that feels overwhelming, and how might expressing gratitude for God's presence in this uncertainty change your experience of waiting from endurance to expectation?

Week 23: Grateful for Imperfect Families

"Accept one another, then, just as Christ accepted you, in order to bring praise to God."

(ROMANS 15:7)

The Roman church was a diverse group of people who couldn't quite figure out how to get along. Jewish Christians and Gentile Christians brought different traditions, expectations, and ways of doing things into their new community. Family dynamics often mirror those same tensions.

Your family probably doesn't look like the ones in holiday commercials where everyone smiles around a perfect table. Real families include the uncle whose politics turn dinner sour, the sibling who still pushes your buttons, or the parent whose expectations never match your reality.

Paul's instruction to accept one another as Christ accepted us hits differently when applied to family. Christ accepted you while you were still making mistakes. He saw your potential while loving your present reality, flaws and all.

Being grateful for imperfect families means acknowledging that these relationships, with all their complications, are often where we learn the deepest lessons about unconditional love. Your family members know your worst habits and your most annoying traits, and they are still your family. That's not a curse; it's a strange kind of grace.

The grace found in imperfect families is that they give you realistic expectations for all your other relationships. Relatives become the training ground for the kind of acceptance Paul describes.

This doesn't mean accepting abuse or enabling destructive behavior. Healthy boundaries are often necessary, and sometimes love requires tough conversations or difficult decisions. But it does mean approaching family dysfunction with the awareness that you are just as imperfect as everyone else around the table.

Your family may have left you with scars to sort through, but they also gave you memories that bring comfort and a sense of belonging that doesn't depend on performance.

Paul's goal in acceptance wasn't just harmony but bringing praise to God. Perfect people loving each other perfectly wouldn't be noteworthy. But imperfect people loving each other imperfectly but persistently? That reflects something beautiful about divine love.

If your family relationships are particularly difficult right now, remember that gratitude doesn't require perfection. You can thank God for the way your family has shaped you, even while healing from the places they've hurt you.

This Week's Prayer

God, thank You for the family You gave me, flaws and all.

Some days they stretch me past what I think I can handle.

Other days they love me in ways I don't deserve.

Teach me to accept them the way You accept me. Give me wisdom for boundaries when they are needed and grace when patience runs thin. Thank You for the resilience, love, and lessons I've learned through them. Help me honor You by loving my family even in their imperfection. Amen.

What qualities or lessons has God taught you through the imperfect parts of your family, and how can you thank Him for those today?

How has your family's acceptance of your flaws shown you God's grace, even if they've also hurt or disappointed you?

Which family relationship challenges you most right now, and how might gratitude for that person's place in your life reshape the way you love them?

Week 24: Thank You for Midnight Mercies

"For his anger lasts only a moment, but his favor lasts a lifetime; weeping may stay for the night, but rejoicing comes in the morning."

(PSALM 30:5)

At 3 AM the world feels different. Darkness stretches long, your thoughts grow loud, and small worries become mountains. Psalm 30 promises that those nights don't get the final word.

Yet David also discovered something remarkable: God's mercy doesn't clock out when the sun goes down.

The early morning hours magnify everything. Ordinary concerns turn into disasters in your mind, and your thoughts race through worst-case scenarios that feel overwhelming and inescapable. The absence of light turns molehills into mountains.

Maybe you know these restless hours intimately.

David's promise that weeping may stay for the night speaks to the reality that some pain can't be rushed through or reasoned away. Sometimes you have to sit with the sorrow, feel the full weight of what's broken, and let the tears fall without trying to fix everything immediately. But his assurance that rejoicing comes in the morning isn't just about time passing. It's about God's faithfulness breaking through even the darkest stretches.

God's midnight mercies don't always look like dramatic rescues. Sometimes they arrive as unexpected peace in the middle of panic, a verse that comes to mind precisely when you need encouragement, or the strange comfort of knowing that you're walking through shadow with Him. His mercy might show up as a sudden idea at 3 AM that provides clarity you couldn't find during daylight.

Being grateful for these late-night mercies means recognizing that God's attention doesn't fade when the sun goes down. The same God who paints spectacular sunrises also maintains the stars that shine in your darkest nights.

Your hardest hours might be where you've experienced some of the most intimate encounters with God's character. When everything else is stripped away, that's often where His mercy feels most tangible.

The night David references isn't just the few hours between sunset and sunrise. It's any time in your life when darkness seems to dominate.

Maybe you're in a late-night hour right now, reading these words when sleep eludes you. Thank God that His mercy is available at 3 AM just as surely as it is at noon.

This Week's Prayer

God, thank You for love that never sleeps, even when I can't. When 3 AM finds me wide awake with worry, thank You that Your attention doesn't fade with the daylight. In these dark hours when everything feels overwhelming, help me recognize the ways You show up with comfort, peace, and strength I didn't think I had.

Thank You for midnight mercies that prove Your promises hold weight in real darkness. Give me hope that rejoicing will come in the morning.

Amen.

What midnight mercy or unexpected comfort in a dark moment can you thank God for, and how did it reveal His faithfulness in ways daylight never could?

How has sensing God's presence in your hardest nighttime hours changed the way you understand His love when life feels overwhelming?

What situations feel darker at night than during the day, and how might gratitude for God's constant mercy help you face those hours with more peace?

Week 25: Celebrating Who I Am, Not What I Do

"See what great love the Father has lavished on us, that we should be called children of God! And that is what we are!"

(1 JOHN 3:1)

John could hardly contain his wonder when he wrote these words. 'See what great love!' he bursts out, stunned that the God of the universe calls us His children. It isn't because we've earned it or impressed Him, but simply because His love is that extravagant.

We live in a culture obsessed with productivity and performance. Your worth gets measured by your job title, your income, your achievements, and your ability to check items off endless to-do lists. Scroll through your feeds and the message is clear: you are what you achieve, how fast you move, and how much you produce.

But God's perspective turns this equation upside down.

Before you've completed a single task today, before you've succeeded at anything or failed at everything, you wake up as a beloved child of the Most High God. That's not your goal to achieve. It's your identity to celebrate.

Being grateful for who you are rather than just what you do means acknowledging that your value doesn't fluctuate with your productivity. Your identity remains stable because it's secured in God's unchanging love, not your changing circumstances.

Children don't earn their place in a family by behaving well, and they don't lose it by messing up. They belong because they're family. That's it. God's love works the same way.

This doesn't mean your actions don't matter or that you shouldn't strive for excellence in your responsibilities. But your activities flow from your identity rather than creating it. You work, serve, and create not to become someone valuable but because you already are someone valuable.

Being grateful for your identity as God's child frees you from the pressure to constantly justify your existence through achievement. You can rest at times when productivity isn't possible, and you can try new things without fearing that failure will destroy your worth.

The same God who spoke galaxies into existence calls you His beloved child. That's not hyperbole or wishful thinking. "That is what we are," John insists, as if he can hardly believe it himself.

Today, let gratitude for who you are silence the pressure to prove yourself by what you do.

This Week's Prayer

Father, thank You for lavishing such great love on me that You call me Your child. When I feel pressure to prove my worth through achievements, remind me that my identity was settled the moment You claimed me as family. When performance anxiety tells me I don't belong, remind me that being Your child isn't something I earned or could lose.

Give me the freedom to rest and set healthy boundaries because my worth isn't tied to constant productivity.

Amen.

What accomplishments or roles have you leaned on to define your worth, and how might gratitude for your identity as God's child change how you see them?

How does knowing your value doesn't rise or fall with productivity shape the way you rest, set boundaries, or handle failure, and what part of that can you thank God for today?

Where are you still trying to earn love or approval through performance, and how might celebrating your unchanging identity as God's beloved child transform those relationships?

Week 26: Gratitude for the Work in Progress

"And we all, who with unveiled faces contemplate the Lord's glory, are being transformed into his image with ever-increasing glory, which comes from the Lord, who is the Spirit."

(2 CORINTHIANS 3:18)

Halfway in, reality shows up. The spark of starting has cooled, goals that felt possible now feel out of reach, and patterns begin to surface. Some are hopeful. Others make you wonder if you've changed at all.

Paul knew this tension. He didn't promise quick results. He described transformation as slow, steady, born from attention fixed on Christ rather than yourself.

Maybe you wanted patience but still snap. You hoped to worry less but anxiety still runs the show. You planned to give more but fear holds you back. The gap between who you want to be and who you are can weigh heavy.

Transformation isn't something you force. It happens as you keep turning toward Christ, even in frustration and failure.

Gratitude means noticing small shifts. Choosing calm instead of irritation. Praying instead of spiraling. Forgiving when you'd rather not. These matter.

Your growth may not look like discipline mastered or fear erased. Sometimes it looks like gentleness with yourself when discipline fails. Sometimes it's learning you can live well even while worry lingers. Growth is often persistence more than perfection.

"Ever-increasing glory" points to slow increments. Like a child growing. Invisible day by day, undeniable over years. Seeds planted months ago are already shaping you, even if change feels too subtle to name.

Gratitude also means trusting God sees more than you do. He notices what you miss. He keeps working when you feel stuck.

And it isn't finished. Thank Him that His persistence never depends on yours.

A Short Request

If this devotional has been meaningful so far, would you consider leaving a short, honest review? You can even add a photo or video if you'd like. Your words and reflections help others decide if this book might encourage them too.

This Week's Prayer

God, at this halfway point, thank You for grace that covers both my growth and my failures. Help me see the person I'm becoming and trust that You will finish what You started in me. Thank You for quiet transformation that happens one step, one moment at a time.

Amen.

What area of growth can you see in your life so far, and how can you thank God for that work even if it feels small or unfinished?

Where are you most frustrated with slow progress, and how might gratitude for God's patience shift your perspective on those struggles?

How has your view of spiritual growth changed from expecting quick results to noticing gradual transformation, and what about God's way of working can you thank Him for today?

Real Life Gratitude

Honest thankfulness for imperfect people in imperfect situations

Week 27: Rest for Weary Souls

*"Take my yoke upon you and learn from me,
for I am gentle and humble in heart,
and you will find rest for your souls."*

(MATTHEW 11:29)

Some tiredness goes away with a nap. But then there's the kind that seeps into your bones, the weariness no amount of sleep can fix. That's the kind of exhaustion Jesus was speaking of when He said, "Take my yoke upon you... and you will find rest for your souls."

"Yoke" might sound like more work, but Jesus was describing partnership. In a yoke, the stronger one carries most of the weight while the weaker one learns the rhythm. Jesus invites you into this kind of relationship, working alongside Him rather than striving alone, letting His strength carry what you cannot.

Maybe you've been running on empty so long that exhaustion feels like your normal. But Jesus offers a different perspective: rest isn't the reward for finishing your work. It's the foundation that makes sustainable work possible.

Being grateful for permission to rest means acknowledging that God designed your human limitations not as flaws to overcome but as reminders to depend on Him. Your need for sleep, downtime, and renewal is God's way of telling you that you are not infinite, and you do not have to be.

This rest Jesus promises goes deeper than physical sleep, though that matters too. Soul rest comes from knowing you don't have to earn God's love through performance, and that your worth isn't measured by your productivity. It's the peace that settles over you when you stop trying to be God and start trusting that He actually is.

Rest becomes a spiritual discipline when you practice it intentionally. Every time you choose to stop striving — to hand your worries, health, or future back to God — you're declaring that He is bigger than your to-do list and more capable than your effort. Rest is what happens when you trust that the world won't fall apart if you pause, because the One holding it all together never sleeps.

Maybe your rest looks like saying no to commitments that drain your soul even when they seem important. Perhaps it's taking walks without your phone or letting the dishes wait while you have an actual conversation with your family.

The gentleness Jesus describes in Himself is the same gentleness He wants you to show yourself. He doesn't drive you like a harsh taskmaster but guides you like a kind teacher.

Your permission to rest comes from the One who never grows weary, yet understands completely that you do.

This Week's Prayer

Jesus, thank You for inviting me into rest instead of piling on more burdens. You know how easily I wear myself out, trying to carry more than I should. Teach me when to work and when to stop, when to move and when to restore. Give me peace in the quiet moments I often resist.

Thank You that Your yoke is easy, and that walking with You brings a rest I could never find on my own. Help me receive that rest with gratitude today. Amen.

What fears or beliefs about rest have kept you from receiving it as a gift, and how can you thank God for designing your limits as invitations to lean on His strength?

How might seeing rest as spiritual discipline instead of laziness change your view of Sabbath, and what's one way you can practice grateful rest this week?

Where are you carrying burdens that belong in Jesus' yoke instead of on your shoulders, and how can you thank Him for inviting you to share that load?

Week 28: Thank You for Messy Kitchens and Full Hearts

"Where there are no oxen, the manger is empty, but from the strength of an ox come abundant harvests."

(PROVERBS 14:4)

You might think a clean kitchen means you're doing life right. But look closer: the dishes in the sink, coffee grinds on the floor, the sauce left on the stovetop after last night's meal. They're proof of something better. People gathered at your table. Laughter ran late. Stories were shared over seconds. Solomon said the same about oxen: no mess, no harvest.

Life forces us to choose between sterile perfection and productive chaos.

Your home tells a story too. Toys scattered across the living room, books piled on every surface, and laundry that never seems finished might feel like failures, proof that you're not managing well enough. But they can also be reminders that love is being lived out in real time.

Maybe you've been apologizing for your home in the same way, pointing out the clutter, excusing the mess, and trying to prove you're on top of it. But what if these signs of chaos are actually signs of love, proof that life is happening, even if it's messy?

Being grateful for messy kitchens and full hearts means choosing to see your chaos through God's eyes rather than through the lens of picture-perfect ideals. You're acknowledging that the most beautiful lives are often the most complicated ones, that love creates beautiful disorder.

The oxen in Solomon's proverb represent strength, productivity, and life force. But they also represent daily responsibilities, ongoing needs, and yes, regular messes. You can choose the empty manger of a perfectly controlled life, but you'll miss the abundant harvest that comes from embracing the beautiful complexity of relationships and service.

Wisdom knows the difference between life-giving mess and soul-draining disorder.

Maybe your gratitude practice needs to expand beyond the Instagram-worthy moments to include the real evidence of love in action. Your messy kitchen and full heart might be exactly the life God designed for you right now.

The mess requires daily care, but it's also what makes the harvest possible.

This Week's Prayer

Father, I confess that too often I've been embarrassed by the evidence of real life in my home instead of grateful for it. Thank You that You see the love behind every pile of laundry, the care behind every cluttered counter, and the grace in every unfinished task.

Teach me to see dishes, toys, and crumbs not as failures but as signs of people, provision, and connection. When perfectionism whispers that I'm falling short, remind me that You measure abundance differently than the world does. Give me eyes to see mess as mercy and hearts as full. Amen.

What "messes" in your life actually represent abundance and meaningful engagement that you can thank God for instead of apologizing for?

How has pursuing perfection over fullness robbed you of gratitude for the beautiful chaos that meaningful relationships and purposeful work naturally create?

What signs of life being lived fully in this stage of your life can you celebrate today, and how might embracing these instead of hiding them deepen your contentment?

Week 29: Finding Grace in Chaos

"Therefore do not worry about tomorrow, for tomorrow will worry about itself. Each day has enough trouble of its own."

(MATTHEW 6:34)

The kingdom of God doesn't always appear in grand gestures. Sometimes it hides in the smallest details, waiting for eyes willing to notice. Jesus pointed to children as our example because they know how to stop, stare, and marvel at what grown-ups rush past.

He spoke these words to people drowning in fear about the future. Rather than promising to erase their problems, He offered something better: peace in the middle of chaos by focusing on today's portion of grace instead of tomorrow's imagined disasters.

When life feels like it's spinning out of control, gratitude can seem impossible. Real disruptions shake the ground beneath you, creating fear that can't be dismissed with clichés or positive thinking.

Yet Jesus shows that even in genuine chaos, peace is still possible. It comes not from controlling everything but from narrowing your focus to what's actually in front of you right now. The weight of tomorrow doesn't belong on your shoulders today.

Being grateful for grace in chaos doesn't mean you're thankful for the chaos itself. It means recognizing God's presence within it. Even when life feels unmanageable, today carries the strength, wisdom, and resources you need for this moment. Tomorrow's challenges will come with tomorrow's grace. Spending today's energy on tomorrow's worries only depletes what you need now.

Maybe your chaos looks like juggling multiple urgent needs, each one shouting for attention. The sheer volume leaves you paralyzed. But Jesus invites you to practice what feels like radical tunnel vision: What truly needs your attention today? What one step can you take right now? This isn't denial of the bigger picture but a way to keep tomorrow's fears from hijacking today's peace.

Grace in chaos often looks ordinary. A sudden calm when panic should have the upper hand. A moment of clarity about your next step. A reminder that you're not carrying this alone. God's peace doesn't wait for perfect conditions; it slips in quietly, right where you are.

Your chaos doesn't surprise Him or outrun His provision. Today's grace is enough for today's challenges, and tomorrow's grace will meet tomorrow when it arrives.

Peace comes when you stop trying to solve everything at once and start receiving God's grace one moment at a time.

This Week's Prayer

God, when life feels overwhelming and my thoughts race ahead to every possible disaster, teach me to breathe and focus on today.
Thank You that Your grace arrives in daily portions, always enough for what I face right now. Help me stop borrowing tomorrow's troubles and instead receive today's mercy with gratitude. When my responsibilities pile up and I feel paralyzed, show me the next small step I can take.

Thank You for peace that finds me in the middle of chaos.

Amen.

What situation feels so overwhelming that you've been borrowing anxiety from tomorrow instead of focusing on today, and how can you thank God for today's specific grace?

Where have you experienced unexpected peace or clarity in the middle of chaos, and what do those moments reveal about God's presence with you?

How might practicing gratitude for today's challenges instead of tomorrow's possibilities change the way you experience stress and trust God's provision?

Week 30: Grateful for Bodies That Carry Us

"Do you not know that your bodies are temples of the Holy Spirit, who is in you, whom you have received from God? You are not your own; you were bought at a price. Therefore honor God with your bodies."

(1 CORINTHIANS 6:19-20)

Most of us know what it's like to have a complicated relationship with our bodies. We've criticized them, compared them, or wished they worked differently. Paul's words cut through all of that, reminding us that our bodies are not accidents or afterthoughts but sacred dwellings of the Spirit, worthy of honor and care.

He first wrote these words to people in a culture obsessed with appearance and indulgence. Some Corinthians treated their bodies as irrelevant to spiritual life, while others elevated physical pleasure above everything else. Paul pointed them toward a better vision: seeing their bodies as holy spaces where God Himself chooses to live.

Your relationship with your body probably holds a challenging history. Maybe you've criticized the mirror, apologized for taking up space, or felt betrayed when illness or injury set limits you didn't want. But what if you began to see your body through God's eyes instead of your own?

Being grateful for the body that carries you means recognizing it as more than a mistake or burden. It's the vessel that has carried you through joy and hardship, strength and weakness, resilience and change.

This doesn't mean ignoring health concerns or pretending physical limitations don't matter. It means beginning from gratitude instead of disappointment.

Paul's temple imagery suggests both reverence and responsibility. You don't worship your body or center your worth on it, but you also don't neglect or abuse it. You care for it as sacred. Honoring your body may mean eating to fuel instead of punish, moving in ways that bring joy instead of striving for impossible ideals, resting when rest is what it truly needs. Every act of care becomes stewardship of what God entrusted to you.

Your body is the only one you'll have in this life. It has carried you faithfully through every experience so far. And the Holy Spirit has chosen to dwell within it, this imperfect, aging, sometimes frustrating body. If God finds it worthy of His presence, perhaps you can find it worthy of gratitude and care too.

This Week's Prayer

Father, help me see this body You gave me through Your eyes rather than the world's expectations. When I'm tempted to focus on what I wish were different, redirect my attention to the wonder of Your design. Thank You for lungs that breathe without my permission, a heart that beats faithfully through stress and sleep, muscles that adapt and strengthen when I ask them to do more. Help me stop measuring this temple by the world's standards and start appreciating it by Your design. When I'm frustrated by limitations or changes, remind me that every body tells a story of grace.

Amen.

What specific ways has your body faithfully served you that you can thank God for today, even if it doesn't look or function the way you wish?

How might shifting from criticism to gratitude change your daily relationship with your body and the way you care for this temple God has given you?

What would it mean to honor God with your body not by chasing perfection but by treating it with the dignity of a sacred dwelling place of the Holy Spirit?

Week 31: Laughter is a Gift From God

"Our mouths were filled with laughter, our tongues with songs of joy. Then it was said among the nations, 'The Lord has done great things for them.'"

(PSALM 126:2)

There are moments when gratitude can't stay quiet, when the only fitting response is laughter. That's what happened when God's people returned from exile. After years of sorrow and silence, joy broke loose in a way that words alone couldn't hold.

Deep laughter can provide relief that no amount of logic or willpower achieves. Your body literally relaxes, your perspective shifts, and for precious moments you remember that not everything in life requires serious attention. God designed laughter as both release and restoration.

Maybe laughter feels scarce in your current circumstances. Life has handed you situations that demand seriousness and attention. When everything feels overwhelmingly weighty, the capacity for genuine joy can seem like a luxury you can't afford or don't deserve.

But laughter isn't frivolous. It's functional. It's one of the ways God restores your soul when weariness threatens to overtake you. Those moments when something strikes you as absurdly funny are gifts of grace arriving precisely when you need them most.

Being grateful for laughter that heals means acknowledging that joy and sorrow can coexist without canceling each other out.

Sometimes the healing power of laughter comes through community: shared jokes that become family legends, or friends who know exactly how to make you smile when life feels heavy. Other times it arrives in solitary moments when something strikes you as funny and you realize you're still capable of lightness despite everything you're carrying.

The nations noticed Israel's laughter because it was evidence of transformation. People who have genuine reasons for sorrow can still experience authentic joy, and it points to something beyond human resilience. It reveals the presence of a God who helps you with laughter when things feel impossible.

Your laughter might be testimony to others watching your life, wondering if faith makes any real difference in how people handle difficulty.

This doesn't mean forcing cheerfulness when you feel sad or pretending problems don't exist. But it does mean remaining open to moments of unexpected delight and trusting that God uses even laughter as part of His healing work.

This Week's Prayer

God of joy, thank You for the gift of laughter that does what medicine cannot do and reaches places that logic cannot touch. Help me remain open to joy without guilt, knowing that laughter doesn't minimize my struggles but strengthens me for them. Thank You for the times when my joy becomes testimony to others that You really do restore what seems broken.

Amen.

What recent moment of genuine laughter can you thank God for, and how did that experience provide relief or perspective you needed during a stressful time?

How has sharing laughter with others deepened your relationships and reminded you of God's goodness in ways that serious conversations alone couldn't accomplish?

Where in your life do you need healing that laughter might provide, and how can you remain open to moments of unexpected joy without feeling guilty about experiencing lightness during difficult circumstances?

Week 32: Celebrating Ordinary Moments

"And he said: 'Truly I tell you, unless you change and become like little children, you will never enter the kingdom of heaven.'"

(MATTHEW 18:3)

Jesus spoke these words to adults who had forgotten how to see magic in the mundane. They had grown serious about important things and lost their capacity for wonder about simple things. While they debated who was greatest in the kingdom, children nearby were probably fascinated by shadows on the ground, delighted by discoveries adults would have dismissed as trivial.

Watch a child encounter a butterfly and you'll see the kingdom perspective Jesus described. They don't analyze its species or worry about whether watching it counts as productive. They simply marvel at the unexpected beauty that appeared in their ordinary day.

Maybe you've trained yourself out of noticing small delights because adult life demands attention to bigger concerns. The constant pressure of "adulting" can blind you to the small wonders right in front of you.

But Jesus suggests that entering His kingdom requires rediscovering this childlike capacity for celebration. Not naïve denial of your real, everyday problems, but wonder that finds reasons for joy even while problems remain. A child can cry over a scraped knee and, minutes later, beam with excitement over a shiny rock. Gratitude for ordinary moments is a practice of kingdom vision, finding adventure hidden in the mundane.

This shift doesn't call for different circumstances, but a different kind of attention. Through adult eyes the day appears routine. Through childlike awareness it brims with quiet treasures: the feel of your favorite coffee mug warming your hands, the steam curling upward with its fragrant invitation, the sound of your dog settling into sleep.

Children find adventure because they approach life with curiosity instead of duty. They ask questions adults stopped asking. Everything holds potential for discovery when nothing is written off as boring.

Slowing down to notice these simple moments is not wasted time. It is training your heart to receive the kingdom as Jesus described it. Gratitude grows when you pay attention to details most people overlook, and in that paying attention you begin to experience the presence of God woven into ordinary rhythms.

Maybe your ordinary moments are invitations to practice kingdom living right where you are, celebrating instead of enduring. Heaven's kingdom isn't only a future destination but a present reality available to those who keep childlike eyes for wonder.

This Week's Prayer

Jesus, help me recover the childlike wonder I've trained myself out of in pursuit of adult seriousness. When I rush past small beauties because they seem insignificant, slow me down to notice what You are revealing in ordinary moments. Teach me to see Your presence in the details I usually overlook and to welcome the joy You scatter through my day. Thank You for hiding adventure in mundane experiences and for filling my routine with reasons to celebrate. Help me practice gratitude for the kingdom moments that show up right in front of me.
Amen.

What ordinary moment from this past week contained wonder or beauty that you initially overlooked, and how might approaching similar experiences with childlike curiosity change your daily gratitude?

How has adult seriousness about important responsibilities caused you to miss opportunities for celebration and joy in routine experiences, and what would it look like to balance both perspectives?

Where in your regular weekly routine could you practice kingdom vision that finds adventure in the mundane, and what specific ordinary moments might God be inviting you to celebrate rather than simply endure?

Week 33: Grateful for Hard Conversations

"Better is open rebuke than hidden love. Wounds from a friend can be trusted, but an enemy multiplies kisses."

(PROVERBS 27:5-6)

Most of us would rather do almost anything than have a hard conversation. We dodge calls, change subjects, and convince ourselves that silence is kinder. But Proverbs reminds us that honesty, though uncomfortable, is often the truest form of love.

Hard conversations rarely feel like gifts while you are having them. Your heart pounds as you gather courage to address concerns. Words stumble when stakes are high, and you wonder if honesty will cost you the relationship.

Avoidance feels easier than risking conflict.

Yet these difficult exchanges often become turning points that deepen trust and create space for authentic connection.

Solomon reminds us that withholding truth out of "love" usually protects our comfort, not the other person's well-being. Hidden love spares us awkwardness but leaves others without what they need. Enemies flatter because they don't care enough about our growth to risk our disapproval.

Being grateful for hard conversations means recognizing that courage to speak truth comes from God and that He can use these moments to strengthen relationships.

Wisdom matters too. Timing, tone, and motive shape the outcome. Words spoken in anger wound differently than words spoken in love. Good intentions do not guarantee good results, but avoiding necessary conversations almost guarantees missed opportunities for deeper connection.

Sometimes you will be the one receiving hard truth. Gratitude in those moments means seeing feedback as a gift rather than a threat. People who care enough to risk your displeasure are offering something of real value.

Not every conflict requires confrontation, and discernment is key. But when relationships matter and the issue is significant, honesty guided by love builds something stronger than superficial peace.

These conversations test the strength of relationships. Trust deepens when people prove they can face hard truths together without walking away.

This Week's Prayer

God, give me courage to have important but uncomfortable conversations. Help me know when love means speaking hard truths and when to remain silent. Thank You for friends who challenge me with honesty and for relationships strong enough to handle it.

Teach me to receive feedback with humility, speak truth with love, and choose timing and words wisely. Help me value real connection over easy peace, even when it feels risky. Amen.

What hard conversation have you been avoiding that might actually serve love better than silence, and how can you thank God for the chance to show care through honesty?

How has receiving difficult but necessary feedback from someone who cared about your growth changed your view of the value of "wounds from a friend," and what about that experience can you be grateful for today?

What relationships in your life have been strengthened by surviving honest conversations, and how might gratitude for that courage encourage you to choose authenticity over artificial peace?

Week 34: Thank You for Forgiveness

*"For if you forgive other people when they sin against you,
your heavenly Father will also forgive you.
But if you do not forgive others their sins,
your Father will not forgive your sins."*

(MATTHEW 6:14-15)

Forgiveness can feel like one of the hardest commands in Scripture. It cuts against instincts to defend ourselves, demand justice, or hold on to hurt. But Jesus ties it directly to our experience of God's mercy, reminding us that grace is never meant to stop with us.

Jesus connected forgiveness in both directions, receiving it from God and extending it to others, in a way that makes many people uncomfortable. This isn't a transaction where we earn God's forgiveness by forgiving others first. Rather, Jesus reveals that hearts capable of receiving divine mercy naturally overflow with mercy toward others.

Forgiveness might be the most misunderstood spiritual practice in Christian life. We often treat it as a feeling we must manufacture rather than a decision we make regardless of our emotions. True forgiveness doesn't require liking someone who hurt us or pretending their actions didn't matter. It means releasing our right to punish them and entrusting justice to God.

Maybe someone's betrayal still stings when you remember it. Perhaps a family member's harsh words echo in your mind during quiet moments. The natural response involves replaying scenarios where you get even, imagining conversations where you defend yourself perfectly, or harboring resentment that feels justified given what happened.

But carrying these burdens affects you more than it affects them.

Being grateful for forgiveness means acknowledging both the mercy you've received and the freedom that comes from extending it to others. God's forgiveness of you isn't based on your perfection but on His character. In the same way, forgiving others reflects your grasp of grace rather than their worthiness to receive it. Extending forgiveness often feels impossible until you remember how much you've been forgiven.

Forgiveness doesn't happen instantly. It's often a process you must repeat each time the hurt resurfaces. You forgive, then remember the offense and feel angry again, then choose forgiveness again. This cycle isn't evidence that you're bad at forgiving.

The freedom forgiveness brings benefits you more than the person you're forgiving. Resentment binds you to people who hurt you, keeping their negative impact alive in your thoughts and emotions. We forgive because we've been forgiven, not to earn forgiveness.

This Week's Prayer

Father, thank You for forgiving me continually, even when I repeat the same mistakes and struggle with the same weaknesses. When I'm tempted to withhold forgiveness from someone who doesn't seem to deserve it, remind me that I, too, don't deserve Your forgiveness, yet You give it freely. Help me understand that forgiving others doesn't mean excusing their actions or pretending they didn't matter. Thank You for teaching me that forgiveness reflects Your character through the choices I make. Amen.

How has receiving God's complete forgiveness for your own failures changed your willingness to extend mercy to others who have hurt or disappointed you?

What relationship in your life currently needs the healing power of forgiveness, and how can you thank God for the opportunity to reflect His mercy in that situation?

When you think about forgiveness as freedom for yourself rather than just kindness toward others, how does that perspective motivate you to release resentments you've been carrying?

Week 35: Finding Joy and Gratitude in Simple Pleasures

"I know that there is nothing better for mortals than to be happy and to do good while they live. That each of them may eat and drink, and find satisfaction in all their toil—this is the gift of God."

(ECCLESIASTES 3:12-13)

After experiencing every pleasure life could offer, Solomon arrived at a surprising conclusion about happiness. He tried wealth, wisdom, pleasure, and achievement, only to find that none delivered the satisfaction they promised. Yet he didn't decide joy was impossible. Instead, he discovered it hiding in plain sight, found in ordinary moments most people overlook while chasing grand dreams.

The Teacher's insight shifts the focus from chasing extraordinary circumstances to paying extraordinary attention to the everyday.

Our culture often insists that happiness depends on having more money, better circumstances, different relationships, or bigger achievements. But real pleasure is often already here. The warmth of morning sunlight, the first sip of coffee that clears the fog, the comfort of clean sheets after a long day, or laughter shared with people you love. These simple gifts carry the power to satisfy you if you notice them.

Maybe you've been postponing joy. I'll be happy when… But Solomon's wisdom says waiting for perfect conditions often means missing the simple pleasures God offers right now, pleasures that don't rely on anything changing.

Even mundane tasks can become sources of gratitude when you see them as opportunities to contribute and use your abilities for others. The difference between drudgery and contentment often isn't in the work itself but in perspective.

Think about the small joys that sustained you during hard times. They didn't solve your problems, but they offered restoration and space to breathe. That's the kind of satisfaction Solomon points to: ordinary experiences carrying a quiet, lasting richness.

God designed humans to take pleasure in basic experiences that reflect His goodness.

Solomon's reflections on eating, drinking, and finding satisfaction in work reveal a sustainable rhythm of happiness. Work can become worship and meals can become communion, all through thankfulness. This doesn't discourage growth or striving. It invites joy in the process, in the ordinary, in God's everyday gifts.

Thank God today for the simple pleasures and happiness He brings into your life with His love.

This Week's Prayer

God, thank You for showing that joy can be found in simple pleasures scattered throughout ordinary days. Help me notice the gifts You offer now, instead of postponing happiness for future achievements or possessions.

Thank You for the satisfaction in meaningful work, the comfort of rest, and the delight in small daily blessings. Amen.

What simple pleasure from your daily routine brings you genuine joy when you pay attention to it, and how can expressing gratitude for these small gifts change your overall sense of contentment?

How has waiting for circumstances to improve before allowing yourself to be happy prevented you from receiving joy that's already available through ordinary experiences?

What aspects of your regular work or daily responsibilities could become sources of satisfaction if you approached them as opportunities to serve and contribute rather than just obligations to complete?

Week 36: Grateful for the God of Details

"How precious to me are your thoughts, God! How vast is the sum of them! Were I to count them, they would outnumber the grains of sand—when I awake, I am still with you."

(PSALM 139:17-18)

David tried to wrap his mind around something impossible to fully grasp: God thinks about him constantly. Not just occasional check-ins or general awareness, but continuous, detailed attention that exceeds human capacity to comprehend.

We often imagine God as too busy managing the universe to notice our small struggles. Yet David discovered that divine attention operates differently than human attention. It doesn't diminish when divided but somehow encompasses everything simultaneously.

When you're grateful for God's attention to details, you're acknowledging that nothing about your life is too insignificant for His care. The private struggles you haven't shared with anyone else don't escape His notice. He pays attention to your inner world with the same thoroughness He brings to managing the universe, somehow caring deeply about both your personal concerns and global events without either diminishing the other.

Maybe you've hesitated to pray about matters that seem trivial compared to world hunger or war. You feel selfish bringing personal concerns to God when others face life-threatening situations. But this perspective misunderstands both God's capacity and His character. His love doesn't operate like a finite resource that gets depleted when distributed widely.

Consider how human love works in your closest relationships. You don't love your spouse less because you also love your children.

The number of grains of sand David mentions is staggering. Think of endless shorelines, dunes, and deserts stretching beyond what your eyes can see. Try to scoop up even a handful, and you'd lose count before you began. Yet David insists God's thoughts about you outnumber even that.

This detailed divine attention transforms how you approach prayer and daily life. You don't need to present only significant requests. God welcomes your thoughts about frustrating commutes, difficult relationships, financial worries, and career decisions alongside discussions of faith and forgiveness.

Your details matter to God because you're important to Him. The same love that sustains galaxies also notices when you need Him.

Thank God today for attention that encompasses both universal concerns and personal specifics, for love that never grows tired of thinking about you, and for the precious reality that you wake up each day already held in the mind of Someone who knows every detail of your life and cares about each one.

This Week's Prayer

Father, thank You for thinking about me constantly and caring for even the smallest details of my life. Help me remember that nothing is too small for Your notice or too large for Your power. Give me confidence to bring every concern to You and trust in Your attentive love.

Amen.

What specific small detail of your daily life can you thank God for noticing and caring about, even though it might seem insignificant compared to larger world issues?

How does knowing that God's thoughts about you outnumber grains of sand change your willingness to bring both major concerns and minor frustrations to Him in prayer?

When you consider that you wake up each morning already held in God's detailed awareness, how might this truth transform your sense of significance and your approach to starting each day?

Week 37: A Morning of Love and Grace

"Satisfy us in the morning with your unfailing love, that we may sing for joy and be glad all our days."

(PSALM 90:14)

The first light through your curtains carries more than brightness. It brings a breath of possibility, a quiet reminder that night has ended. Steam curls from your morning cup, and for a moment the day feels gentler. The table may still hold yesterday's clutter, but the new day arrives anyway, carrying mercy with it. Moses prayed to wake satisfied by God's love, because he knew mornings weren't just hours on a clock. They were fresh chances for joy.

Maybe yesterday ended in regret. Words you can't take back. Choices that haunt you more in the silence of night than they did in the noise of the day. That heaviness can make waking feel like a punishment instead of a gift. Yet God doesn't weigh your worth with yesterday's failures. His love isn't on trial.

To wake with gratitude is to admit that God's constancy doesn't hinge on your record. His love isn't volatile, reacting to your moods or missteps. Morning arrives carrying the same care He's always had for you.

It's steady, unaffected by the chaos of the day before.

Still, renewal doesn't mean erasure. Mistakes leave marks. But the new day opens space for different choices. A tense conversation can guide you toward gentler words next time. A plan abandoned last week can be picked up again, this time with clearer sight.

For some, mornings don't feel light at all. Responsibilities pile up before the coffee is poured. Stress greets you faster than sunlight. That's real. And still, Moses' prayer points us to something deeper: joy that comes not from a perfect life but from love that meets you the minute your eyes open, before anything else gets a say.

Notice what happens when a day begins with gratitude rather than dread. Same schedule, same to-do list, but you walk into it differently. Less from deficit, more from abundance.

God provides the fresh start, but you decide whether to take it. That often means forgiving yourself, loosening your grip on yesterday's anger, and allowing room for new possibilities. It doesn't always look dramatic. More often, it looks like choosing again, quietly.

Morning after morning, God's love waits for you. Not earned. Not delayed until you're worthy. Already present. Already holding you. That love doesn't solve every problem, but it does make facing them possible.

So maybe today, thank Him for the sunrise. For mercy that keeps showing up. For love that never grows tired of beginning again with you.

This Week's Prayer

God, thank You for mornings filled with mercy instead of judgment. When regret or worry wakes with me, remind me that Your love doesn't shift with my failures. Teach me to receive each day as a fresh start, and to extend that same grace to others. Let gratitude shape how I move through the day. I don't want to miss Your kindness. Keep my heart steady in Your love.
Amen.

How does starting each morning with gratitude for God's fresh mercy change your ability to handle mistakes and setbacks throughout the day?

What specific area of your life needs the hope that comes from daily fresh starts, and how can you thank God for new opportunities to grow rather than feeling defeated by past failures?

When you consider that God's love arrives each morning before you've done anything to earn or lose it, how does this truth affect your sense of worth and your approach to the day ahead?

Week 38: Celebrating Progress, Not Perfection

"Let us not become weary in doing good, for at the proper time we will reap a harvest if we do not give up."

(GALATIANS 6:9)

The Galatians were tired. They'd been faithful for so long, trying to do good in a world that seemed determined to pull them backward. The results they longed for never appeared as quickly as they hoped, and the weight of that gap wore them down. Paul's reminder is simple but disruptive: growth doesn't work on instant timelines. It moves at the pace of seeds in soil.

We know that feeling. You work on patience for months, then snap again when stress runs high. You promise yourself consistency in prayer, but it slips through your fingers. Finances, habits, relationships — you see where you want to be, but reality feels like it's dragging behind. The distance between intention and outcome can look unbearable.

But progress isn't always dramatic.

Sometimes it's a pause before anger, even if the next day you still lose your temper. It's three days of prayer that mattered, even if the fourth was missed. It's an argument that ends with listening instead of slamming the door. Every wise choice, however small, stacks into something more.

Much of what God is forming in you is invisible. Roots going deeper. Character stretching quietly. Our culture teaches us to measure by speed and visibility. Scripture pushes us to measure by faithfulness.

The problem is we keep looking for transformation to arrive in one grand sweep. We want prayer to feel powerful every time, patience to click into place overnight. But God values the tiny shifts we barely notice. These are the small movements that accumulate over years.

Maybe you're already different and haven't realized it. Conflicts that once exploded now end more calmly. Forgiveness doesn't feel as impossible as it used to. Generosity comes easier. None of it is perfect. All of it is progress.

Paul speaks of a harvest "at the proper time." That time isn't ours to decide. Farmers can't rush weather or soil any more than we can dictate the pace of spiritual maturity. Our part is to keep sowing.

Weariness sets in when we expect results too quickly. Gratitude steadies us when we start noticing the movement that's already here. Today, thank God for the changes that seem small but signal real growth. Trust that the hidden work will one day break the surface.

This Week's Prayer

God, help me celebrate progress instead of despairing over how far I still have to go. When discouragement comes from trying without seeing results, remind me that growth follows Your timing, not mine. Thank You for small steps that matter even when I dismiss them. Give me eyes to notice the hidden work You're doing beneath the surface. When I'm tempted to give up, steady me with hope. Teach me to keep showing up with gratitude, trusting You for the harvest. Amen.

What area of spiritual growth can you thank God for, even though you haven't reached your ultimate goal, and how might celebrating that progress motivate continued faithfulness?

How has expecting immediate results from persistent effort led to discouragement, and what would change if you approached personal growth with agricultural patience rather than instant gratification expectations?

When you look back over the past year, what positive changes in your character or choices can you identify that deserve celebration, even if they feel small or incomplete?

Week 39: Grateful for Grace in the Storm

*"Who shall separate us from the love of Christ?
Shall trouble or hardship or persecution or famine
or nakedness or danger or sword?"*

(ROMANS 8:35)

Every life collects storms. Some are sudden: the phone call, the diagnosis, the betrayal. Others grind slow: years of financial strain, broken relationships, or decades of unanswered prayers.

Paul doesn't deny these storms. He names them, then insists they cannot undo God's love.

Gratitude feels impossible when suffering refuses to leave. The weight of loss presses down until even breathing feels like betrayal.

Yet Paul penned these words while chained to a Roman guard, his body marked by persecution. He wasn't theorizing about suffering; he was living it.

And from that place of raw pain, he dared to ask the question that leads to one answer: nothing can separate us from Christ's love.

The Greek word Paul uses for "separate" describes a permanent disconnection. But here's what Paul learned in his darkest moments: God's love isn't conditional on our circumstances being easy.

This is where gratitude gets redefined. We're not thankful because life is easy; we're thankful because love is unshakable.

Paul's list reads like a catalog of human nightmares: trouble that leaves you gasping, hardship that steals your sleep, persecution that makes you question everything, famine that empties your cupboards, nakedness that strips away dignity, danger that makes you look over your shoulder, even the sword. He's not sugar-coating reality or pretending faith makes life painless.

But here's the radical truth that changed everything for Paul: God's love isn't just stronger than our suffering; it's present within it.

This kind of gratitude doesn't deny pain. It transforms it.

Standing in the wreckage of what was supposed to be, we can whisper a different kind of thanks.

Thank You that this dark time doesn't define me. Thank You that this failure doesn't disqualify me. Thank You that this broken place doesn't break Your love for me. Thank You that when I have nothing left to give, I still have everything that matters: Your unshakable, unfailing, unending love.

This Week's Prayer

Father, when life hits me with wave after wave of trouble and my faith feels fragile, hold me in this truth: nothing can separate me from Your love. When hardship makes gratitude feel impossible, help me remember that I'm grateful that pain can't touch Your heart toward me. Thank You that even when I can't feel Your presence, I can trust Your promise. Even when I can't trace Your hand, I can trust Your heart. You love me in the valley just as fiercely as You love me on the mountaintop.

Amen.

What current hardship is challenging your ability to feel grateful, and how might remembering God's unshakeable love shift your perspective on that situation?

When has God's love felt most real to you during a difficult period, and what specific ways did you experience His presence in that pain?

Looking back on past valleys you've walked through, how has your understanding of gratitude deepened or changed through suffering?

Deep Roots of Thankfulness

Unshakeable hope that weathers any storm

Week 40: Thank You for Lessons in Disguise

> "Blessed is the one who perseveres under trial because, having stood the test, that person will receive the crown of life that the Lord has promised to those who love him."
>
> (JAMES 1:12)

Have you been in a situation where failure felt suffocating? You poured in effort, but the outcome never matched. Everything you built seemed to crumble anyway.

Yet in the silence that followed, you found a firmer foundation than success could ever give. You didn't want that lesson. You didn't like the way God taught it. But you learned.

James uses a word for "trial" that means testing authenticity, like a jeweler putting gold under heat. The point isn't destruction. It's to reveal what's genuine beneath the surface. Your hardest lessons weren't random cruelty from an uncaring universe. They were invitations to discover your true composition.

Perseverance isn't teeth-gritting or forcing yourself through. Sometimes it's rising one more morning when staying in bed feels easier. Sometimes it's asking for help when pride screams you should manage alone.

Here's what James grasped that's easy to miss: trials don't just test your faith, they transform it. Before that long stretch of hardship, you may have believed God was good because life was easy.

After walking through fire, you know He is good even when life feels anything but. That kind of faith can't be learned in a classroom.

The crown of life is the existence that emerges from being refined.

Maybe the fire is still burning. Maybe you're looking back at a time that almost broke you, noticing glimpses of purpose only now. Either way, gratitude doesn't have to be for suffering itself, only for how God carries you through the struggle.

Not one moment is wasted.

Every tear, every sleepless night, every step you thought you couldn't take becomes part of a story only you can tell. Your healing becomes hope.

So whisper a different kind of thanks. Thank You for supporting me in the valley. Thank You for not letting the fire consume what matters most. Thank You for lessons I never wanted but needed. Thank You for turning the worst chapters into something still beautiful.

This Week's Prayer

Father, it's hard to be grateful for times that nearly broke me, but I'm learning to thank You for how You are there for me. When I wanted to quit, You gave me strength for one more day. You've turned even my hardest experiences into something meaningful.

Help me see the lessons You've been teaching through difficulty, and give me wisdom to share what I've learned with others who are struggling. When I'm tempted to resent the fire, remind me that it revealed a strength I never knew I carried. Amen.

What difficult experience in your life initially felt like pure loss but eventually taught you something valuable you wouldn't have learned any other way?

How has walking through a hard period of time changed the way you relate to God, and what aspects of His character did you discover in the darkness that you might have missed in easier times?

Looking at your current struggles, what might God be teaching you now that could one day become a lesson of hope for someone else?

Week 41: Grateful for Changing Perspectives

"Do not conform to the pattern of this world, but be transformed by the renewing of your mind. Then you will be able to test and approve what God's will is—his good, pleasing and perfect will."

(ROMANS 12:2)

A detour you never would have chosen felt like wasted time until it revealed God's presence and shifted your focus to what truly matters.

Paul's words landed in a city obsessed with power, spectacle, and success, a Rome humming with idols and distractions. Different century, same relentless pressure.

How you see the world changes everything. It shapes the stories you tell yourself and the goals that keep you up at night. Maybe for years you tied worth to promotions or possessions. Then something cracked that system. The numbers stopped adding up, and what once defined success no longer satisfied.

Paul calls this a transformation: not a self-help adjustment or a positive spin, but a mind rewired, rebuilt, by God's truth.

That renewal is rarely instant.

Each day requires choices. You can drown in fear, or you can remember the voice that calls you beloved. You can chase distraction, or you can sit quietly with words that steady you.

The shift can feel jarring. What used to excite you leaves you restless, and the goals you thought would prove your value lose their shine. But what seemed like loss becomes space for God to fill with better desires and deeper joy.

Perspective doesn't always flip overnight. Sometimes it comes like dawn; gradual until suddenly the whole sky is light. Other times it's like lightning, one sharp break that changes everything at once.

A renewed mind doesn't erase difficulties. The bills still arrive, and people still disappoint. But what once felt like proof of failure can become the ground where trust takes root. Even uncertainty, instead of consuming you, starts to open space for faith to breathe.

Slowly, God's will feels less like a riddle and more like a path you're already walking. Gratitude grows in this space: not only when things go right, but in the very twists you once resented.

This Week's Prayer

Lord, I confess I resent the shifts you bring. I'm tired of unlearning the familiar patterns, and I still desperately cling to the comfort of lies I've outgrown. Forgive my resistance. Thank you for not letting me stay stuck, and thank you for the moments when you shatter my narrow view and let me glimpse your true priorities, even though it wrecks my old way of seeing. When the pressure to conform mounts, and fear starts writing the story, wrench me back to the truth of who you are and who I am in you. Give me fierce patience for this slow, day-by-day work of renewal, and the vicious courage to trust that you're reshaping me even when I feel empty and lost. Let your will become a path I want to walk.

Amen.

What specific "detour" or perspective shift has most dramatically changed how you approach life, and what circumstances catalyzed that change?

How has renewing your mind with God's truth helped you exchange a source of stress or anxiety for the ground where trust can take root?

In what area of your life do you still find yourself conforming to the world's patterns, and what specific *choice* can you make today to invite God to transform that perspective?

Week 42: Finding God in the Darkness

"If I say, 'Surely the darkness will hide me and the light become night around me,' even the darkness will not be dark to you; the night will shine like the day, for darkness is as light to you."

(PSALM 139:11-12)

Have you ever felt the crushing disconnect between God's clear promise and your current reality? David did. He was meant to be a king, yet he was hiding in caves, living in the tension of a future he couldn't see.

Sound familiar?

Life has a way of scrambling your internal compass just when you need direction most. What looked like answered prayer six months ago now feels like a mistake you can't undo. Every assumption you'd made about the next chapter gets rewritten by events that seem to contradict everything you thought God was telling you.

These situations feel like walking through thick fog with a broken flashlight. Every step forward is uncertain, and every decision carries weight you're not sure you can bear.

But David discovered something powerful during his years of confusion and waiting: God's vision doesn't depend on your ability to see clearly. While you're stumbling through uncertainty, He's seeing the entire landscape with perfect clarity.

Maybe you're standing at a crossroads right now, paralyzed by too many options or devastated by too few. Perhaps major changes have been thrust upon you. These upheavals can make you feel like you're free-falling through space with no idea where you'll land.

God's perspective during your most disorienting moments becomes a gift worth treasuring. While your teenager's rebellion rocks your foundation, He sees the young adult they're becoming, not just the chaos they're creating. Financial setbacks might feel like failure, but He recognizes opportunities for trust and provision you can't yet imagine.

That sense of being completely lost often precedes breakthroughs in ways you'd never expect.

Your current confusion doesn't indicate God's absence. It reveals an invitation to trust His navigation when yours fails completely. He sees around corners you haven't reached yet and illuminates paths that are invisible to you right now but will become obvious once you start walking deeper in faith.

The darkness that overwhelms you is simply another kind of daylight to the One who holds your future.

This Week's Prayer

Lord, I confess my terror when the fog rolls in and I can't see the next step. I hate the feeling of being paralyzed by choices or devastated by the loss of certainty. My heart screams that You've forgotten me here. Thank You that Your sight is the light I don't have. Wrench my focus onto your light, not the darkness I feel. Give me the simple courage to take the next breath, believing that what is night to me is still daylight to You. Amen.

What current area of confusion or uncertainty in your life might be an invitation to trust God's guidance more deeply than relying on your own understanding?

Looking back at a previous stretch of time when life felt chaotic and unclear, how can you now see God's hand working even when you couldn't recognize it at the time?

How might your experience of working through dark, confusing moments equip you to offer hope and practical wisdom to others facing similar disorientation?

Week 43: Thank You for Imperfect Celebrations

"Every day they continued to meet together in the temple courts. They broke bread in their homes and ate together with glad and sincere hearts."

(ACTS 2:46)

We all know the shame of rushing to hide the laundry before a guest rings the bell. But the early church never faced that pressure. Their joy flowed from something so much deeper than elaborate staging or a clean house.

Social media wasn't there to document every perfectly arranged detail for public approval or make you feel inadequate about your table settings. These early Christians simply opened their doors, shared their meals, and created sacred space through presence rather than presentation.

Maybe you've cancelled that gathering because the house wasn't clean enough, postponing connection until circumstances are ideal.

This impulse to wait for ideal conditions often robs us of the very relationships our souls crave most desperately.

God seems to specialize in using our flawed attempts as foundations for genuine connection. When your carefully planned dinner party falls apart, pride gets set aside and real conversation begins. Guests stop performing their best selves and start connecting with your actual self when they realize you're refreshingly human too.

The early church's "glad and sincere hearts" weren't dependent on external circumstances aligning perfectly. Their joy flowed from being together, sharing life in all its messy reality while focusing on what truly mattered.

Your grandmother's kitchen table, scarred by years of family meals, witnessed more meaningful conversations than most five-star restaurants ever will. Those surface imperfections told stories of love lived daily.

Maybe it's time to stop waiting for the perfect moment to invite people into your actual life.

Those early believers broke bread together daily. They didn't have endless resources but they did recognize something vital about human design. We're created for connection.

Your crooked cake says "I tried" in ways that store-bought perfection never could. A morning coffee shared over a mismatched mug or paper plates and pizza shared with genuine warmth create memories that elaborate presentations served with stress can never match.

The early church changed the world not through perfect hospitality, but through hearts that were perfectly glad to be together.

This Week's Prayer

Father, when I'm tempted to wait for ideal circumstances before opening my home and heart, remind me that love matters more than presentation. Thank You for friends and family who gather around my imperfect table with grace, who see past the burned edges and mismatched dishes to the heart behind the effort. Give me courage to invite people into my real life, not just my polished one. Amen.

What perfectionist tendencies have prevented you from hosting gatherings or inviting people into your life, and how might letting go of those standards create space for deeper connection?

When has an "imperfect" celebration or gathering become one of your most treasured memories, and what made that experience so meaningful despite its flaws?

When you think about friends who truly understand you without requiring explanation, what particular acts of their understanding or support can you thank God for today, and how might expressing that gratitude deepen those relationships?

Week 44: Grateful for What Didn't Happen

"In their hearts humans plan their course, but the Lord establishes their steps."

(PROVERBS 16:9)

You planned, you prayed, you tried. So why did the door slam shut?

Solomon's perspective on divine guidance came through decades of experiencing both granted and withheld prayers. His later writings reveal a man grateful not just for what God granted, but for what divine wisdom withheld.

That job you desperately wanted but didn't get still stings when you remember the rejection letter. Six months later, when the company made massive layoffs, you began to glimpse God's protective hand in what felt like abandonment.

What looks like divine neglect from one angle appears as divine protection from another.

Sometimes God's greatest gifts come wrapped in disappointment. The graduate school rejection that forced you to reconsider your career path entirely seemed like the end of your dreams until it led to discovering talents you never knew existed, revealing a calling that fits your heart in ways the original plan never could have.

This unexpected detour often leads to a shift in self-trust. You stop relying on your own limited vision and start relying on the One who closes the door. The sting of rejection fades into the sweet realization that God's redirection preserved something vital—your peace, your purpose, or even your soul—from a future you couldn't handle on your own.

God establishes your steps even when you can't feel His guidance, especially when His path diverges from your preferred route.

Maybe you're wrestling with disappointment right now, confused about why certain doors keep slamming shut. These closed paths might feel like evidence of God's indifference. But Solomon learned this truth: human hearts make plans based on limited information, while divine wisdom sees the entire story. God knows what opportunity would derail His better purpose for your life.

Your current frustration with unanswered prayers might be tomorrow's testimony of God's perfect timing.

This Week's Prayer

Father, it's hard to be grateful for disappointments that still hurt, but I'm learning to trust Your protection even when it feels like rejection. Thank You for the job I didn't get that would have demanded my soul, the relationship that didn't work out that would have settled for less than Your best. Help me see Your loving hand in closed doors and redirected paths. When I'm frustrated by circumstances that don't fit my plans, remind me that You see dangers I cannot imagine and opportunities I'm not yet ready to handle. Give me faith to trust Your timing over my urgency, Your wisdom over my understanding.

Amen.

What disappointment or closed door in your life has revealed itself over time to be divine protection rather than divine neglect?

How might your current frustrations with unanswered prayers or blocked paths be preparing you for something better than what you originally wanted?

Looking back at your life's trajectory, where can you see God's hand redirecting you away from paths that seemed appealing but would have led to complications or harm?

Week 45: Celebrating Hope That Endures Long Waits

"Not only so, but we also glory in our sufferings, because we know that suffering produces perseverance; perseverance, character; and character, hope. And hope does not put us to shame, because God's love has been poured out into our hearts through the Holy Spirit, who has been given to us."

(ROMANS 5:3-5)

We usually pray for an escape from suffering. Paul prayed to glory in it. He knew that the hope that endures isn't found in a quick fix, but slowly, painfully forged through years of unanswered prayers and circumstances that tested how God truly works.

Paul penned these words while imprisoned, his ministry stalled and freedom uncertain. Yet he writes about glory not despite suffering, but because of what suffering produces in the waiting. His view of hope was forged through years of unanswered prayers and circumstances that tested every assumption about how God works.

Waiting feels like the cruelest teacher, demanding patience you don't possess while offering lessons you never wanted to learn. That prayer you've been praying for five years still echoes in empty rooms, seemingly unheard by heaven. The longing in your heart grows deeper rather than dimmer with time, making you wonder if hope is just foolishness dressed up in spiritual language.

But Paul discovered something transformative about hope during his times of uncertainty: it isn't diminished by delay but refined by it. Like waiting for the kettle to boil while the exhaustion of the morning weighs on you, the hope that comes from waiting bears little resemblance to the wishful thinking that characterizes our prayers.

Maybe you're in the middle of a wait that feels endless right now. Suspended animation teaches you things about faith and fear that comfortable times never could.

The character Paul mentions isn't built through easy victories or quick answers to prayer. It develops slowly. It wasn't in the victories that your character formed, but in the nights you wondered if God was listening and still chose to trust. That quiet defiance against despair became the foundation for your strength.

Paul's progression from suffering to perseverance to character to hope isn't a timeline but a transformation. Each time of waiting doesn't just test what you already possess; it creates qualities that couldn't exist without the pressure.

Your current wait might feel like punishment or evidence that your prayers lack power. But what if this delay is actually developing something in you that instant answers could never produce?

Real hope is about committing your trust to the God who refuses to abandon you, no matter how unclear His plan feels right now.

This Week's Prayer

Lord, I confess I resent this cruel teacher called waiting. My faith feels foolish, and my hope is fragile under this endless delay. Forgive me for measuring Your love by the speed of Your answer. Help me find the holy defiance to trust Your goodness even when my timeline collapses. Thank You for building perseverance in the hollow spaces where my expectation failed. Amen.

How has an extended period of waiting in your life developed character qualities or spiritual depth that you wouldn't have gained through quick answers to prayer?

What's the difference between hope and expectation in your current situation, and how might shifting from expectation to hope change your experience of waiting?

Looking back at previous times of prolonged waiting, how can you see God's love and faithfulness at work even when His timeline didn't match your preferences?

Week 46: Thank You for Chaotic Love

"Consider it pure joy, my brothers and sisters, whenever you face trials of many kinds, because you know that the testing of your faith produces perseverance."

(JAMES 1:2-3)

The sound of your children arguing over dinner is not usually mistaken for pure joy. Yet John, the apostle of love, knew that true affection is rarely tidy. He witnessed the love of Jesus, a mixture of tender care and hard truth, shaped not by flawless moments but by the stumbles and recoveries of human hearts.

His understanding of love grew from the messy reality of people learning to reflect God's love while still being gloriously, frustratingly human. This is the honest, everyday love God pours out for us too.

Your kitchen table bears witness to love that looks nothing like greeting card sentiments: dinner conversations interrupted by homework disputes, affection expressed through packed lunches made at dawn while you're barely awake, and devotion shown by staying up late to help with projects you don't understand.

Maybe you've apologized to your children more times than you can count for losing patience when exhaustion drowned out grace. The guilt feels heavy because you know they deserve better, and your love for them burns fiercely even when your delivery falters. But what if this imperfect love, offered sincerely and repaired faithfully, is teaching them something invaluable about grace?

John reminds us that love originates from God, not from our ability to express it flawlessly. Every attempt to love, however incomplete, connects us to the divine source that keeps pouring itself through cracked vessels.

The tangled beauty of family love mirrors something sacred about God's affection for us. He doesn't wait until we become worthy recipients; He loves us while we're still learning and stumbling toward forgiveness.

Think of the night when you snapped at your spouse during a stressful week, then sat down later to sort through what went wrong and how to make it right. That cycle of failure and repair might be the most godlike thing you do. Divine love doesn't ignore wounds; it acknowledges them honestly and works toward healing.

John's simple command to "love one another" acknowledges that love is both a divine gift and a human choice, supernatural in origin but natural in expression.

Thank God for love that looks like chaos but feels like home.

This Week's Prayer

Father, I feel the guilt of my imperfect love every day. My patience fails, my words are clumsy, and I snap when I should show grace. Forgive the distance between my intention and my execution. Thank You for showing me that Your love flows through willing hearts rather than perfect ones. Give me the courage to stay close and risk the beautiful, messy disasters that come with truly loving others.

Amen.

How has your imperfect but persistent love for someone in your life become a source of growth and grace for both of you?

What would change in your relationships if you focused on loving abundantly rather than loving perfectly?

Where can you see evidence of God's love flowing through your ordinary, chaotic acts of care for the people in your life?

Week 47: Grateful for New Beginnings

*"I will give you a new heart and put a new spirit in you;
I will remove from you your heart of stone
and give you a heart of flesh."*

(EZEKIEL 36:26)

How many times have you tried to reform yourself, only to watch your resolutions crumble?

Who told you there's an expiration date on your new beginning?

Ezekiel's voice rose among a people who believed God had turned away, their spirits too cold to respond to grace.

Yet God promised a transformation so complete it would be like receiving a new heart, trading stone for flesh and numbness for life.

That pattern you've been trapped in for years feels like your identity, rather than the prison you could walk free from. You react before you even realize it, and your best intentions seem to vanish under pressure.

Maybe you've tried to change countless times, making resolutions that lasted weeks instead of months.

But something shifted when you finally stopped trying to manufacture transformation through willpower alone and started asking God to do what you couldn't do for yourself.

God's promise doesn't require you to forget your old life or pretend your losses don't matter. He offers transformation that honors your past while opening futures you can't yet imagine. That stone heart, developed as protection during years of disappointment, becomes the foundation He builds upon, not the obstacle He works around.

Maybe you're convinced your fresh start expired decades ago. God's timeline for new beginnings operates on different principles than society's expectations. The new spirit He promises isn't just about positive thinking; it's receiving divine breath that animates possibilities you'd written off as impossible.

Your heart of stone developed through necessity, protecting you from further damage. But what fulfilled its purpose as armor during devastating times can become a prison during healing ones. God's gentle surgery removes those protective barriers that no longer fulfill their purpose.

Sometimes new beginnings look less like dramatic overhauls and more like subtle shifts in perspective that change everything. God's promise to make your heart flesh means you get to feel deeply again without fear of being destroyed by the feeling.

It's never too late for a new heart.

This Week's Prayer

Father, when I feel too worn or too damaged for fresh starts, remind me that Your promise of new hearts never expires. Thank You for seeing potential where I see only disappointment and for gently removing the hardness that keeps me from trusting. Give me courage to step into the beginnings You offer, even when they look different from what I expected. Thank You for being the God who constantly restores.

Amen.

What area of your life feels "set in stone" that God might be inviting you to see as an opportunity for fresh beginnings?

How might past disappointments or losses have created protective barriers in your heart that no longer fulfill their purpose, and what would it look like to allow God to soften those places?

Looking at your current life stage, what new beginning might God be offering that you've dismissed as impractical or impossible due to your age or circumstances?

Week 48: Maintaining Hope When Life Feels Stuck Or Broken

"Be strong and take heart, all you who hope in the Lord."

(PSALM 31:24)

Real hope isn't the optimistic belief that everything will work out exactly as you want it to. It is the deep confidence that you are held by Someone whose love remains constant regardless of how your current chapter unfolds.

David's words ring with the authority of someone who had learned to hope in the darkness, not just in the light. He ends his lament not with despair but with this rallying cry to anyone else walking through their own valley of shadows. His hope wasn't based on circumstances improving quickly, but on the unchanging character of the One who holds all our chapters together.

You've been living in what feels like the difficult middle of a story that refuses to move toward resolution. The situation that seemed temporary six months ago has settled into permanent residence in your daily reality. Every morning brings another day of the same financial stress, relational tension, or health concerns that rob sleep and steal your peace.

Maybe you're wondering if this particular struggle is your new life rather than a temporary detour.

But David's command to "take heart" suggests that hope is both a gift we receive and a choice we make daily. Some mornings hope feels as elusive as trying to grasp morning mist with your bare hands. Other days it burns steady and strong, carrying you through challenges that would have overwhelmed you in weaker moments.

The strength David mentions isn't the kind that powers through problems with gritted teeth and stubborn determination. It's the kind that comes from remembering who has walked through darkness before you and who promises to walk through it with you now.

Perhaps the hardest part of living in difficult chapters is how they affect your perspective on everything else. Even small decisions feel monumental when your internal resources are stretched thin.

Yet these challenging times often reveal reservoirs of strength you didn't know existed within you.

Take heart today, because the God who holds your story specializes in writing redemption into plots that seem destined for defeat.

This Week's Prayer

Father, when this hard chapter feels endless and hope seems like a luxury I can't afford, remind me that You specialize in stories that appear impossible to redeem. Thank You for walking through difficult times with me instead of simply rescuing me immediately. When my strength fails and my perspective narrows to the present pain, help me take heart in Your unchanging character rather than my shifting circumstances.

Give me grace to hope imperfectly and to trust You even when I can't find Your hand in my situation. Thank You that these hard chapters aren't proof of Your absence but opportunities to discover Your presence in ways I never knew possible. Help me remember that You are the Author of my story, and You have never written an ending that doesn't reflect Your goodness. Amen.

How has living through a prolonged difficult period of time changed your understanding of what it means to hope in God rather than hope in circumstances?

What evidence of God's faithfulness from past hard chapters can you draw upon to take heart in your current struggles?

In what ways might your current difficult time be developing character qualities or spiritual depth that easier circumstances couldn't produce?

Week 49: Thank You for Faithful Friends

"But Ruth replied, 'Don't urge me to leave you or to turn back from you. Where you go I will go, and where you stay I will stay. Your people will be my people and your God my God.'"

(RUTH 1:16)

Ruth chose to speak to Naomi, whose grief had made her bitter and defensive, pushing away anyone who might help. Naomi's grief had turned her heart sour, convinced anyone near her would inherit disaster. Yet Ruth chose to bind her future to someone who could offer nothing but uncertainty.

You probably know someone like Ruth, a friend who stayed close through your hardest days, even when you gave them every reason to walk away. Their loyalty felt almost unreasonable.

This kind of friendship ignores the usual rules, where people stay only if the benefits outweigh the cost. When your life imploded and you could give nothing back, you saw clearly who was committed to you and who was just around for convenience. The ones who stayed taught you something sacred about love that doesn't depend on reciprocity.

Maybe you think of the friend who came to the emergency room in the middle of the night, who dropped groceries on your doorstep, who listened again and again as you worked through the same fears. Their presence taught lessons about grace that sermons never could, showing what covenant love looks like.

Ruth's choice wasn't impulsive. It was a deliberate intertwining of her story with someone else's, cost be damned. In a culture that prizes independence and self-protection, such commitment feels foreign. Watching it changes how you understand love and how you offer it.

The friend who stays often does so quietly. They keep showing up and believing in your worth when you've forgotten it yourself. Their faithfulness becomes a steady rhythm amid chaos, a heartbeat of hope when your own feels too weak.

These friendships mirror divine love, a love that refuses to give up despite failure and shortcomings. When human friends display this kind of commitment, it becomes a living reflection of how God relates to us. Ruth-like devotion transforms both giver and receiver. Naomi's bitterness softened. Ruth found belonging she could not have predicted.

Your own story was likely made bearable by someone who refused to leave. Their presence didn't solve everything, but it created the support that kept you standing. That faithfulness becomes a treasure, showing you the eternal nature of love.

So thank God today for those who refused to walk away. For the friends who believed in your future when you could not. Friends who showed you through their persistence what a divine relationship looks like. Just like with God, it's loyal, patient, and committed regardless of cost.

This Week's Prayer

Father, thank You for friends who stayed when I gave them every reason to walk away. Through their faithfulness, I glimpse Your heart that never abandons me. Their presence in my darkness reflects unbreakable love in human form. Give me courage to show the same unwavering love to others, even when it costs. May I be a Ruth in someone else's story, choosing loyalty and kindness when it's easier to walk away. Amen.

Who in your life has demonstrated Ruth-like faithfulness by staying committed to your friendship through difficult moments, and how did their loyalty impact your understanding of love?

How has being the recipient of unwavering friendship changed the way you approach your own relationships with others?

In what ways might you be called to show Ruth-like commitment to someone in your life who is currently walking through a difficult time?

Week 50: Grateful for Dreams Deferred

"For the revelation awaits an appointed time; it speaks of the end and will not prove false. Though it linger, wait for it; it will certainly come and will not delay."

(HABAKKUK 2:3)

When you look at your life's vision, does it feel less like a path and more like a stall? Habakkuk lived in a world where everything good was stuck, while the broken parts thrived. He was forced to learn the difference between God's silence and His abandonment.

His words rise from a moment where faith seemed pointless, forcing him to choose trust when timing made no sense.

Think of the project you keep circling back to. A manuscript tucked away. A vision for your life interrupted by bills, exhaustion, or silence. Each time you return, you wonder if you're clinging to something naïve, if "real life" has already buried that dream. The ache of waiting makes it easy to mistake silence for abandonment.

But what if the delay isn't evidence of your dream's death but proof of its importance in God's larger story? The years you've spent away from your manuscript (or whatever your dream is) haven't been wasted time. Instead, you've been gathering experiences and deepening your understanding of human nature. This has taught you lessons about perseverance that will make your dream that much sweeter. The dream deferred has been quietly maturing and developing complexity and depth it couldn't have possessed in your younger, more impatient hands.

Maybe your life doesn't resemble the picture you sketched years ago. Yet what we call postponement, God calls readiness. Skills honed in a "temporary" job may become the backbone of a calling still ahead. Wounds that once cut deep may be the very scars that give your compassion power.

Comparison only sharpens the sting. Friends surge ahead. Doors open for others that remain shut for you. But heaven's timetable isn't measured by competition. The patience forged in waiting might be the very thing that preserves the dream once it arrives.

This waiting isn't passive. Every new skill or idea is shaping you into someone who can carry what once would have crushed you.

Nothing is wasted, even when it feels wasted.

So perhaps today is for holding both grief and gratitude. For admitting the ache of what hasn't come, while trusting that God is still tending what He planted. The delay doesn't mean denial. It means a timing so exact, so full, that one day the waiting itself will look like a gift.

This Week's Prayer

Lord, I confess I resent this delay. The ache of lost time feels like a burden I can't carry, and watching others receive their answers makes my heart shrink. Forgive me for measuring Your faithfulness by their timeline. When I want to give up, remind me that You planted this dream for a reason far beyond my understanding. Teach me not just to endure, but to become strong enough to prepare for the dream when it finally breaks through. Thank You that my dreams deferred aren't dreams denied, but are being prepared for a timing so perfect it will redeem every painful moment of uncertainty. Amen.

How might the delay in fulfilling a particular dream be preparing you in ways that immediate success couldn't have accomplished?

What skills, experiences, or character qualities have you developed during times of waiting that will enrich your dreams when they're eventually fulfilled?

Looking back at previous dreams that materialized later than expected, how can you see God's perfect timing at work in ways you couldn't understand during the waiting period?

Week 51: Celebrating the God Who Stays

"Jesus Christ is the same yesterday and today and forever."

(HEBREWS 13:8)

When your entire world is turned upside down, where do you find the one thing that doesn't move? The original readers of this letter were refugees, watching their temple crumble and their leaders scatter, yet they were anchored by one constant: Jesus Christ.

Their leaders were scattered, and their future uncertain. Yet in the midst of this upheaval, they're reminded of One constant that no earthly crisis could touch.

Your life probably looks nothing like it did five years ago, shaped by changes you never saw coming and losses you never imagined surviving. This relentless pace of change teaches you to treasure constancy in ways that stable times never could.

Everything familiar gets stripped away, and you find the comfort of knowing that Jesus remains exactly who He's always been. He's the same whether you're succeeding or failing, whether your faith feels strong or fragile. His character doesn't fluctuate.

Maybe you're walking through a transition right now that feels like losing your footing on shifting sand.

But Christ's unchanging nature means that your worth doesn't depend on roles you've outgrown or abilities that may be diminishing. The love that held you when you were young and strong holds you just as securely when you're older and tired and carrying scars from battles you never wanted to fight.

The "yesterday and today and forever" promise offers stability when everything else feels uncertain. While technology advances at breakneck speed and cultural values shift like weather patterns, Jesus remains the same compassionate healer who touched lepers and spoke the truth with gentleness.

Perhaps what you need most today is permission to stop trying to adapt to every change and instead rest in the One who never changes.

His unchanging love means you don't have to earn His attention through perfect behavior or maintain His approval through flawless performance. The grace that saved you initially continues to sustain you daily, unaffected by your mood swings and unchanged by your occasional lapses in faith.

The stability Christ offers isn't the kind that prevents change from happening, but the kind that holds you steady while change swirls around you.

Thank God for being the constant in your story of constant change.

This Week's Prayer

*Lord, when everything around me shifts like sand and I can't find solid ground, thank You for being the one constant I can count on.
Your love for me doesn't change when my circumstances change, or when my ability to see Your goodness gets clouded by current struggles.
When I'm tempted to find security in things that can be taken away, hold my heart in Your unchanging nature that no crisis can touch.
Help me rest in Your constancy rather than exhausting myself trying to control variables beyond my influence.*

Amen.

In what areas of your life have you been seeking stability from sources that naturally change, and how might finding your security in Christ's unchanging nature bring peace?

How has experiencing significant life changes helped you appreciate God's constancy in ways you might not have understood during more stable times in your life?

What specific aspects of Christ's unchanging character bring you the most comfort when you're facing uncertainty or transition?

Week 52: Thank You for Grace That Never Ends (and Caffeine, too)

*"And God is able to bless you abundantly,
so that in all things at all times, having all that you need,
you will abound in every good work."*

(2 CORINTHIANS 9:8)

Some days your faith is held together by grace, and your body is held together by caffeine. Paul knew what it meant to run on empty. After shipwrecks, beatings, and jail time, he discovered a secret supply: divine grace that was never theoretical, but experiential and absolutely certain.

He could declare with absolute certainty that God's grace never runs out. His assurance was born from years of witnessing divine supply exceed human demand.

You've no doubt experienced periods when you felt like you were running on empty. Emotionally depleted, spiritually dry, and physically exhausted from demands that seemed to outpace your ability to meet them.

Human logic suggests that constant giving should lead to inevitable depletion, that pouring yourself out repeatedly should leave you empty and unable to continue serving others. Yet you've found that the more grace you receive from God and extend to others, the more grace becomes available to you.

This challenges everything we know about scarcity.

Maybe you're wondering right now if you have enough grace left for the challenge you're facing. The ongoing demands of life make you feel like you're constantly overdrawing from accounts that should have been emptied long ago.

But Paul's promise suggests that God's ability to bless abundantly isn't limited by your current capacity or constrained by your past failures. The grace that saved you initially continues to sustain you daily, multiplying to meet whatever needs arise.

Perhaps what's most remarkable about divine grace is how it transforms the giver as much as the receiver. Every act of forgiveness you extend despite being hurt makes forgiveness easier the next time. Each moment of patience you offer somehow creates more patience for future situations.

The abundance Paul describes isn't primarily about accumulating blessings but about experiencing sufficiency that allows you to bless others freely.

So as this year concludes, thank God for grace that proved sufficient for every day you've lived, every challenge you've faced. Oh, and thank You for caffeine, too!

This Week's Prayer

Gracious God, thank You for grace that flows without end, meeting me in weakness and lifting me in strength. When I felt empty, You filled me. When I faced more than I could bear, You carried me through. As this final week of a yearlong journey closes, let gratitude shape my heart and guide my steps forward. Your supply never runs dry, and for this I give thanks. Help me end this devotional with deep gratitude. Amen.

Looking back on this year, where have you seen evidence of God's proving sufficient for challenges that initially seemed beyond capacity to handle?

How has receiving abundant grace from God changed your ability to extend grace to others, even in difficult relationships or circumstances?

What specific "good works" has God's grace enabled you to accomplish this year that you couldn't have done in your own strength?

Thank you for reading

I hope you loved this devotional as much as I enjoyed writing it. These devotions came from my heart to yours, and I cherish knowing how they've touched your life.

I truly appreciate your support and the time you've taken to read this book. If you feel called to, please leave a review so other Christians can enjoy this devotional. Your words also help me as an author to inspire as many people as I can. Reviews don't have to be long, even a few sentences sharing your experience with the book make a big difference. You can also include a photo or video!

You can leave your review here: http://links.wingsofgracepublishing.com/gratitude-devotional or use the QR code below:

What's Next?

Congratulations on completing this devotional experience! The prayers, reflections, and Scripture passages you've engaged with over these weeks have begun a meaningful transformation in your relationship with gratitude and with God.

If this devotional has resonated with you, I invite you to explore my series, *"From Worry to Worship."* The book and devotional are designed to help you on God's path to living free from anxiety, worry, and stress

You can find them, and all of my books, on my Amazon author page. This is the link: https://www.amazon.com/author/graceandrews

Get your FREE email mini-course 'The Grace-Filled Life'

As a thank you for purchasing this devotional, I would love to gift you with a powerful 7-day mini-course on trusting and living in God's grace absolutely FREE! It will automatically be delivered to your inbox.

You'll find it here:

https://wingsofgracepublishing.com/daily-grace/

or use the QR code below:

Join My Book Launch Team

Want to be part of something special?

I'm looking for amazing readers to join my book launch team. As a team member, you'll get early access to new books and devotionals, behind-the-scenes updates, and the chance to help spread the word about books that matter.

It's simple, fun, and it would be such a blessing to have you as part of the process. If you want to help my books and devotionals reach more hearts, I'd love to have you on the team.

Head to **https://wingsofgracepublishing.com/join/** to learn more and join us!

About the Author

Grace Andrews is a Christian author passionate about sharing the transformative power of faith through inspirational writing. With a heart for spiritual growth, she offers readers practical insights and biblical wisdom to help them navigate life's challenges.

She is fueled by coffee and the love of her husband of 25 years. She adores international travel, quiet moments with God, reading, and creating.

Grace believes that God's love and guidance can lead anyone to greater peace, purpose, and fulfillment.

Find out more about Grace and her books here:

https://wingsofgracepublishing.com/

www.ingramcontent.com/pod-product-compliance
Lightning Source LLC
Chambersburg PA
CBHW072020070526
44583CB00015B/1562